The Fun and Easy MEMORY Activity Book for Adults

Includes Relaxing Memory Activities, Easy Puzzles, Brain Games and More

By J.D. Kinnest

LOMIC BOOKS

The Fun and Easy MEMORY Activity Book for Adults

Includes Relaxing Memory Activities, Easy Puzzles, Brain Games and More

By J. D. Kinnest

ISBN: 978-1-988923-10-9
Published by Lomic Books
Kitchener, Ontario

Copyright

Disclaimer

Table of Contents

Table of contents continued...

Fun memory
games and puzzles
this way!

Introduction

This book provides a fun way to exercise your memory!

In fact, within these pages you will find a wonderful selection of activities, puzzles and games which target different memory and brain skills.

Short-term Memory

Short-term memory is active when a person remembers new information for a few minutes to complete a specific task.

In this book, there are several memory games to exercise your short-term memory including the following:

- **Delightful Details:** In this memory game, you take a look at picture, then turn the page, where you see an almost identical picture, where a detail needs to be filled in.
- **Particular Pictures:** In this game, there are three pictures which you try to memorize. Then you turn the page, and pick out the items from a selection of pictures related to the same theme.
- **Backwards:** In this quick and light memory game, the goal is to write a set of popular sayings backwards.

- **Lovely Lists:** In this short-term memory game, there is a list of related items that you take some time to memorize. Then, you turn the page and pick out the items from a grid of words.
- **The Memory Challenge:** In this memory game, there is a short list of unrelated items you try to memorize in order; then turn the page and write out the items.

By working on these puzzles, you can gently exercise your short-term memory in a fun way.

Long-term Memory

Long-term memory is active when a person recalls information from the past — whether they first committed the information to memory a few weeks ago or a few decades ago.

In this book, there are several memory games that exercise your long-term recall including the following:

- **Cool Categories:** In this long-term memory game, you write as many items you can think of that belong in a specific category.
- **Writing About Your Life:** The goal is to recall and describe past experiences in this long-term memory activity.
- **Rhyme Time:** In this memory puzzle, you use your long-term memory to recall words that rhyme with the word that is "given."

By combining these puzzles, you can gently exercise accessing your long-term memory in an enjoyable way.

Classic Puzzles & Brain Games

We've added a great selection of classic puzzles and brain games to this memory activity book for two reasons:

1. **Many classic puzzles actually exercise either short or long term memory.** For example, crossword solvers use long-term memory to answer clues; while word search solvers use short-term memory to hold a word in their mind while they search for it in the letter grid.

2. **Classic puzzles and games provide a great variety of activities to keep this book interesting.** By combining memory specific activities with classic puzzles and brain games, there is an excellent variety of activities throughout the pages of this book.

So what are the classic puzzles and brain games can you find in this book? Well, they include:

- **Word Searches**
- **Spot the Odd One Out**
- **Find the Differences**
- **Sudoku**
- **Well Made Words**
- **Crosswords**

These delightful puzzles and games provide a relaxing way to get some mental exercise.

Entertaining & Useful Features

This book has several unique features that make it particularly entertaining and useful.

- **Fun Themes.** In this book, each section has a different theme to keep the memory games and puzzles fresh and interesting. For example, some of the themes include "Lovely Vacations" and "Great Gardening."
- **Large Print.** There is large print throughout the book to make it easy on the eyes.
- **Clear Images.** Large and easy-to-see images help put the focus on puzzle solving, not eye strain.
- **Easy-to-use Solutions.** The solutions to the puzzles and activities in this book are designed to be easy to access and understand.

The features listed above make using this book a relaxing and pleasant experience.

Have Some Fun!

The Fun and Easy Memory Activity Book for Adults is meant to be an entertaining way to exercise your short-term memory and long-term recall.

We hope that you have hours of fun working through the pages of this book!

Section One

Memory Activities, Puzzles, and Brain Games

Television & Movies

Includes Delightful Details, Rhyme Time, Cool Categories, Particular Pictures, Writing About Your Life, Trivia Matching, Backwards, Word Search, Crossword, Sudoku, Find the Differences, Odd One Out and The Memory Challenge

RHYME TIME

In this activity, the goal is to write down words that rhyme with the specific "given" word. Take some time to think of as many words as you can.

List words that rhyme with "STAR"

_______________ _______________ _______________
_______________ _______________ _______________
_______________ _______________ _______________
_______________ _______________ _______________
_______________ _______________ _______________

List words that rhyme with "SHOW"

_______________ _______________ _______________
_______________ _______________ _______________
_______________ _______________ _______________
_______________ _______________ _______________
_______________ _______________ _______________

Solution on page 128

Delightful Details

1. Take a look at the picture to the right. On the next page is an identical picture, that is missing one detail. When you are ready, turn the page and fill in the missing detail.

Turn the page to continue

2. Take a look at the picture to the right. On the next page is an identical picture, that is missing one detail. When you are ready, turn the page and fill in the missing detail.

Turn the page to continue

These two puzzles are continued from the previous page.

1. Have you studied the picture on the previous page? Great! Now draw in the one detail that will make the image to the right, identical to the image on the previous page.

Draw in the 1 missing detail!

From the previous page

2. Have you studied the picture on the previous page? Great! Now draw in the one detail that will make the image to the right, identical to the image on the previous page.

Draw in the 1 missing detail!

From the previous page

Solution on page 128

PARTICULAR PICTURES

Take a look at the three pictures below. Take your time to memorize the three items. Then turn the page and pick out the three items that you memorized.

Turn the page to continue

This puzzle is continued from the previous page.

PARTICULAR PICTURES..... CONTINUED

Did you study the three items on the previous page? Great! Now circle the three items that you memorized.

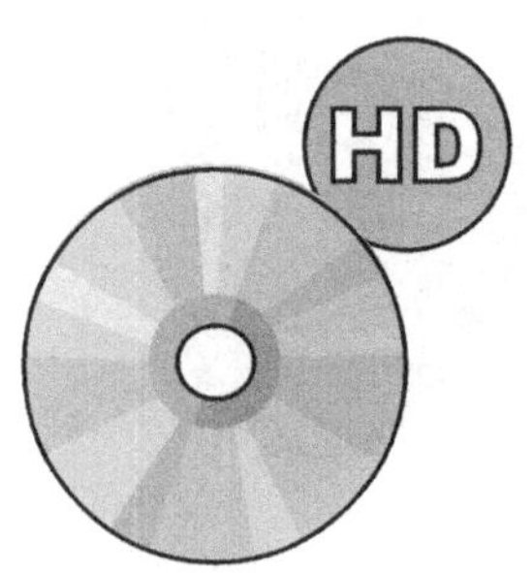

Solution on page 128

Cool Categories!

Make a list of TV shows that are comedies. How many can you think of?

1.
2.
3.
4.
5.
6.
7.
8.
9.
10.
11.
12.
13
14.
15.
16.
17.
18.
19.
20.
21.
22.

Make a list of famous movie actors. How many can you think of?

1.
2.
3.
4.
5.
6.
7.
8.
9.
10.
11.
12.
13
14.
15.
16.
17.
18.
19.
20.
21.
22.

Solution on page 128

Classic Puzzle

CROSSWORD

In this puzzle, write the answer to each clue in the crossword grid. One letter goes into each square.

ACROSS

1) It interrupts a TV show
6) A curve shape
8) ___ Landers, advice columnist
9) 'The ____ Tyler Moore Show'
10) Fuel for a car
11) Home to a bear
12) What we breath
13) Restore health
15) Female deer
17) Had a meal
19) Lease an apartment
20) Place to store a car
22) Lucille ____, comedian
24) 'Fly ___ the wall'
25) Melted fat
27) It makes honey
28) 'Be ____ for the course'
29) A ride on a plane
32) 'A Hard Day's ___,' movie
35) Place to see a movie
36) 'A hard row ___ hoe'
37) 'Big ___,' a clock tower

DOWN

1) Show that makes one laugh
2) 'The Ides of _____'
3) ______ Regan, actor who became US President
4) _____ Bergman, starred in Casablanca
5) Famous TV dog
6) _____ Warhol, artist
7) Sweet treat
14) Opposite of west
16) Yellow and red combined
18) Playfully make fun of
19) ____ McEntire, country singer
20) Bride's partner
21) Day before a holiday
23) Acquire knowledge
26) Opposite of fake
28) Story line
29) It wears a shoe
30) To seize quickly
31) 'Every now and _______'
33) Obtain
34) '____ with the same brush'

1		2			3		4		5	■	6		7
	■		■	■		■		■	8			■	
9				■		■	10			■	11		
	■		■	■	12			■		■		■	
	■	13	14			■		■		■	■	■	
	■	■		■		■	15	16		■	■	■	■
■	■	■		■	■	■	■		■	■	17	18	
19				■	20					21	■		■
	■	■	■	■		■	■		■		■		■
22		23		■	24		■	25	26				
	■		■	■		■	27			■	■		■
■	■		■	■		■	■	■		■	■	■	■
28			■	■	■	■	■	29			30		31
	■	32		33		34	■		■	■		■	
	■	■	■		■		■		■	■		■	
35							■	36		■	37		

Solution on page 129

TRIVIA MATCHING
MOVIES & ACTORS

In this puzzle, the goal is to match a movie to an actor who starred in that same movie. You can draw a line to match items from the movie column to the actor column, or write your answers below.

MOVIE		**ACTOR**	
1.	*The Godfather*	**A.**	Judy Garland
2.	*The Wizard of Oz*	**B.**	Humphrey Bogart
3.	*Pulp Fiction*	**C.**	Mark Hamill
4.	*Citizen Kane*	**D.**	Al Pacino
5.	*Singin' in the Rain*	**E.**	James Stewart
6.	*Casablanca*	**F.**	Gregory Peck
7.	*The Empire Strikes Back*	**G.**	John Travolta
8.	*Gone With the Wind*	**H.**	Gene Kelly
9.	*It's a Wonderful Life*	**I.**	Clark Gable
10.	*To Kill a Mockingbird*	**J.**	Orson Welles

ANSWERS:

1. ________ **2.** ________ **3.** ________ **4.** ________ **5.** ________

6. ________ **7.** ________ **8.** ________ **9.** ________ **10.** ________

Solution on page 129

Writing about your life...

Describe your all-time, favorite television show. Why did you like the show? Who was your favorite character? Why?

BACKWARDS SDRAWKCAB

In this activity, the goal is to write out the sentence backwards. Try to minimize the number of times you look at the original sentence to increase the level of difficulty of this memory challenge.

1. Elvis has left the building.

Write it backwards: ______________________

2. Your guess is as good as mine.

Write it backwards: ______________________

3. It takes two to tango.

Write it backwards: ______________________

4. The pen is mightier than the sword.

Write it backwards: ______________________

Solution on page 130

WORD SEARCH...

MOVIE SET

Find the words below in the letter grid. Words may be hidden in an across, down, or diagonal direction. Also, the words may be spelled forwards or backwards.

Word List:

LIGHTS	SCRIPT	ASSISTANT
CAMERA	STUDIO	FILM
WARDROBE	EXTRAS	DIRECTOR
LOCATION	PROPS	CREW
ACTOR	SET	CAST

H	Q	T	W	S	W	P	A	E	P	J	E	S	A	U	R
R	M	N	C	C	G	B	N	R	B	Q	W	E	C	Z	Y
O	L	A	R	R	X	C	O	O	A	O	I	T	T	L	N
T	I	T	E	I	V	P	A	S	I	S	R	Z	O	C	C
C	F	S	W	P	S	R	T	S	J	T	A	D	R	X	D
E	T	I	R	T	Y	H	N	V	T	P	A	R	R	J	E
R	S	S	P	R	G	C	A	M	E	R	A	C	T	A	Y
I	U	S	G	I	C	Z	A	Y	B	A	N	U	O	X	W
D	Z	A	L	T	S	T	U	D	I	O	O	R	H	L	E

Solution on page 130

SUDOKU

In this sudoku puzzle, use the numbers 1 to 9 to fill in the grid. To complete the grid, you need follow three rules:

1. Every vertical row has the numbers 1, 2, 3, 4, 5, 6, 7, 8 and 9 only once.
2. Every horizontal row has the numbers 1, 2, 3, 4, 5, 6, 7, 8 and 9 only once.
3. Each 3 by 3 square has the numbers 1, 2, 3, 4, 5, 6, 7, 8 and 9 only once.

	6	9	7	1		3	2	
5	7		2	8	6	4		9
	1	2	9		3	8	7	6
9		4	6	7	8		3	2
7	2	6		4	1	9	5	
	3	8	5	2		7	6	4
2	8	5	4	3	7		9	1
6		7	1		2	5	8	
3	9			6	5	2		7

Solution on page 130

Lovely Lists... Movie Night

In each puzzle, memorize the list and then turn the page and circle the words you remember in the word grid.

Kevin is setting up his living room for movie night. He has a list of items he needs to buy. Once you think you've memorized his list turn the page.

Kevin's List

popcorn	ottoman
beer	chips
DVD	cookies

turn the page to continue

◇◇

Joy is creating a home theatre. She has a list of items she needs to buy to create the movie room. Once you think you've memorized her list turn the page.

Joy's List

speakers	rug
seats	screen
pillows	projector

turn the page to continue

These two puzzles are continued from the previous page.

Kevin's List

Circle the items that you remember from Kevin's list in the word grid to the right.

pizza	fries	cookies
popcorn	tape	nachos
juice	beer	soda
coffee	wings	gum
taffy	VCR	DVD
burgers	ottoman	pretzel
chips	glasses	caramel

Joy's List

Circle the items that you remember from Joy's list in the word grid to the right.

film	receiver	seats
speakers	CD	DVR
cable	pillows	blanket
monitor	remote	lights
rug	guide	screen
trays	cups	curtain
projector	switch	panels

Solution on page 131

FIND THE 5 DIFFERENCES

Find the 5 differences between the two pictures.

Solution on page 131

SPOT THE ODD ONE OUT

Find the picture that is different from the rest.

Solution on page 131

The Memory Challenge

This activity is the hardest of the short-term memory games. Below is a list of seven random words. The goal is to memorize the words, then turn the page, and write the words out in order.

The List:

1. Donkey
2. Apple
3. Car
4. Ticket
5. Cake
6. Bee
7. Shovel
8. House

A HINT... (or how to make this challenge doable)

To help memorize a list of unrelated items, you can use your imagination to make the items more memorable.

For example, if you were trying to remember the list:

A. Rabbit
B. Balloon
C. Spoon

You could imagine..... A rabbit (Item A) hopping along. The rabbit spots a balloon (Item B), and starts chasing the it. When the rabbit catches up to the balloon, the balloon pops, and a giant spoon (Item C) appears!

Consider trying this approach with the list to the left.

Turn the page when you have memorized the items.

Short-Term Memory

This puzzle is continued from the previous page.

The Memory Challenge Continued

Write the eight items you memorized from the previous page in the spaces provided.

1. ____________________ 5. ____________________

2. ____________________ 6. ____________________

3. ____________________ 7. ____________________

4. ____________________ 8. ____________________

Brain Game

Well Made Words

Create words out of the letters provided. You can use each letter only once per word.

Letters

A E V L T G

Words

Solution on page 132

Section Two

Memory Activities, Puzzles, and Brain Games

Family & Friends

Includes Rhyme Time, Particular Pictures, Cool Categories, Writing About Your Life, Backwards, Word Search, Sudoku, Lovely Lists, Spot the Odd One Out, Crossword, and The Memory Challenge

RHYME TIME

In this activity, the goal is to write down words that rhyme with the specific "given" word. Take some time to think of as many words as you can.

List words that rhyme with "DAD"

List words that rhyme with "FRIEND"

Solution on page 132

PARTICULAR PICTURES

Take a look at the three pictures below. Take your time to memorize the three items. Then turn the page and pick out the three items that you memorized.

Turn the page to continue

This puzzle is continued from the previous page.

PARTICULAR PICTURES.... CONTINUED

Did you study the three people on the previous page? Great! Now circle the three people that you memorized.

Solution on page 132

Lovely Lists..... Gifts

In these puzzles, the goal is to memorize the list, and then turn the page and circle the words you remember in the word grid.

Patricia needs to go shopping for holiday gifts. She has a list of items she wants to buy for family and friends. Once you think you've memorized her list, turn the page.

Patricia's List

candle	book
scarf	candy
sweater	frame

turn the page to continue

◇◇

Scott is going to go shopping for holiday gifts. He has a list of items he wants to buy for family and friends. Once you think you've memorized his list, turn the page.

Scott's List

slippers	wine
perfume	pajamas
necklace	bike

turn the page to continue

These two puzzles are continued from the previous page.

Patricia's List

Circle the items that you remember from Patricia's list in the word grid to the right.

mittens	scarf	cookies
candle	ring	pen
flowers	watch	sweater
pants	book	hat
candy	sled	skates
doll	puzzle	frame
shoes	ball	tie

Scott's List

Circle the items that you remember from Scott's list in the word grid to the right.

perfume	poster	pillow
tray	vase	wine
clock	slippers	purse
necklace	lamp	phone
pajamas	socks	bike
belt	chair	TV
mirror	blanket	shoes

Solution on page 133

Cool Categories!

Make a list of names of people you went to school with.

1. __________
2. __________
3. __________
4. __________
5. __________
6. __________
7. __________
8. __________
9. __________
10. __________
11. __________
12. __________
13 __________
14. __________
15. __________
16. __________
17. __________
18. __________
19. __________
20. __________
21. __________
22. __________

Make a list of cities in which any members of your extended family live.

1. __________
2. __________
3. __________
4. __________
5. __________
6. __________
7. __________
8. __________
9. __________
10. __________
11. __________
12. __________
13 __________
14. __________
15. __________
16. __________
17. __________
18. __________
19. __________
20. __________
21. __________
22. __________

SUDOKU

In this sudoku puzzle, use the numbers 1 to 9 to fill in the grid. To complete the grid, you need follow three rules:

1. Every vertical row has the numbers 1, 2, 3, 4, 5, 6, 7, 8 and 9 only once.
2. Every horizontal row has the numbers 1, 2, 3, 4, 5, 6, 7, 8 and 9 only once.
3. Each 3 by 3 square has the numbers 1, 2, 3, 4, 5, 6, 7, 8 and 9 only once.

3		9		5	2	1		8
	6	8	9	4		7	2	3
2	7		6	8	3		4	5
4		5	2		9	8	3	6
8	3	2		1	6	5	7	
	9	7	8	3	5	4		2
9	8	3	1	6	4	2	5	
1		6	5		7	3	8	4
7	5			2	8		9	1

Solution on page 133

FIND THE 5 DIFFERENCES

Find the 5 differences between the two pictures.

Solution on page 133

Writing about your life...

Describe your favorite family event that you attended. Was it a wedding or birthday? Who came? What happened?

best holidays

Complete It!
Famous Sayings

In this memory game, the goal is to fill in the missing word in each popular sayings.

1. A friend in ____________, is a friend indeed.
2. The black _____________ of the family.
3. There's no _____________ like home.
4. The _____________ doesn't fall far from the tree.
5. No man is an _______________.
6. Birds of a ____________ flock together.
7. Don't ____________ the hand that feeds you.
8. Two _____________ are better than one.
9. Absence makes the ______________ grow fonder.
10. Two is _________________, three is a crowd.

Solution on page 133

Classic Puzzle

CROSSWORD

In this puzzle, write the answer to each clue in the crossword grid. One letter goes into each square.

ACROSS

1) Often worn when married
4) Dissolution of a marriage
8) Attached to a foot
9) Fix
10) Long-necked bird
11) Abbrev. for toddler
12) '*Everyone Loves* ________' TV show
14) Nonhuman part of the family
15) Promise made when getting married
16) Assist
17) A bird of prey
19) Past tense of meet
21) Your mom's mom
24) Another word for dad
28) Opposite of urban
29) Used to row a boat
30) Abbrev. for 'also known as'
31) 'All is fair in love and _____'
32) '______ and flow'
34) Resolve an issue
35) '________ balls of fire'

DOWN

1) Member of one's extended family
2) Opposite of day
3) Get ready
4) Another word for father
5) Not occupied
6) 'The end of the ______'
7) Raise up
13) To think or move gloomily
14) Composition made in verse
16) 'Lend a helping ________'
18) Tired dog's breathing
20) What a dog wags
21) Present
22) Decor for the ear
23) 'Bark up the wrong ______'
25) 'Be still my beating ________'
26) 'Tough _____ to hoe'
27) 'An ounce of prevention is ______ a pound of cure'
30) 'My hands ______ full'
33) Used in baseball

1 2 3 4 5 6 7 8 9 10 11 12 13 14 15 16 17 18 19 20 21 22 23 24 25 26 27 28 29 30 31 32 33 34 35

Solution on page 134

BACKWARDS SDRAWKCAB

In this activity, the goal is to write out the sentence backwards. Try to minimize the number of times you look at the original sentence to increase the level of difficulty of this memory challenge.

1. A trouble shared is a trouble halved.

Write it backwards: ____________________

2. Home is where the heart is.

Write it backwards: ____________________

3. Too many cooks spoil the broth.

Write it backwards: ____________________

4. Wonders will never cease.

Write it backwards: ____________________

Solution on page 134

WORD SEARCH...
FAMILY

Find the words below in the letter grid. Words may be hidden in an across, down, or diagonal direction. Also, the words may be spelled forwards or backwards.

Word List:

MOM	DAD	NEPHEW
PAPA	UNCLE	TWINS
AUNT	NIECE	COUSIN
SISTER	HUSBAND	PARENT
WIFE	NANA	SON

N	J	W	F	F	R	I	Q	H	D	I	E	L	C	N	U
B	A	U	N	T	A	M	U	B	S	V	E	C	E	I	N
T	V	N	S	B	W	S	D	T	N	R	E	T	S	I	S
H	P	T	A	E	B	G	Y	O	C	N	A	T	I	F	C
C	J	Z	H	A	Y	F	S	N	N	I	P	N	D	P	H
H	W	P	N	T	W	I	N	S	W	S	A	E	P	E	C
J	E	D	J	D	V	M	K	T	F	U	P	R	X	F	P
N	T	H	A	P	O	K	D	T	K	O	N	A	T	I	E
Y	F	D	M	M	P	S	T	I	K	C	H	P	G	W	K

Solution on page 134

SPOT THE ODD ONE OUT

Find the picture that is different from the rest.

Solution on page 135

The Memory Challenge

This activity is the hardest of the short-term memory games. Below is a list of seven random words. The goal is to memorize the words, then turn the page, and write the words out in order.

The List:

1. Tooth
2. Ice Cream
3. Cat
4. Road
5. Cup
6. Chair
7. Tree
8. Sweater

A HINT... (or how to make this challenge doable)

To help memorize a list of unrelated items, you can use your imagination to make the items more memorable.

For example, if you were trying to remember the list:

A. Rabbit
B. Balloon
C. Spoon

You could imagine..... A rabbit (Item A) hopping along. The rabbit spots a balloon (Item B), and starts chasing the it. When the rabbit catches up to the balloon, the balloon pops, and a giant spoon (Item C) appears!

Consider trying this approach with the list to the left.

Turn the page when you have memorized the items.

This puzzle is continued from the previous page.

The Memory Challenge Continued

Write the eight items you memorized from the previous page in the spaces provided.

1. ____________________
2. ____________________
3. ____________________
4. ____________________
5. ____________________
6. ____________________
7. ____________________
8. ____________________

Brain Game

Well Made Words

Create words out of the letters provided. You can use each letter only once per word.

Letters

M I L B E T

Words

____________________ ____________________
____________________ ____________________
____________________ ____________________
____________________ ____________________
____________________ ____________________
____________________ ____________________
____________________ ____________________

Solution on page 135

Section Three

Memory Activities, Puzzles, and Brain Games

Great Gardening

Includes Delightful Details, Rhyme Time, Cool Categories, Particular Pictures, Writing About Your Life, Lovely Lists, Backwards, Spot the Odd One Out, Word Search, Sudoku, and The Memory Challenge

RHYME TIME

In this activity, the goal is to write down words that rhyme with the specific "given" word. Take some time to think of as many words as you can.

List words that rhyme with "SOIL"

List words that rhyme with "TREE"

Solution on page 135

PARTICULAR PICTURES

Take a look at the three pictures below. Take your time to memorize the three items. Then turn the page and pick out the three items that you memorized.

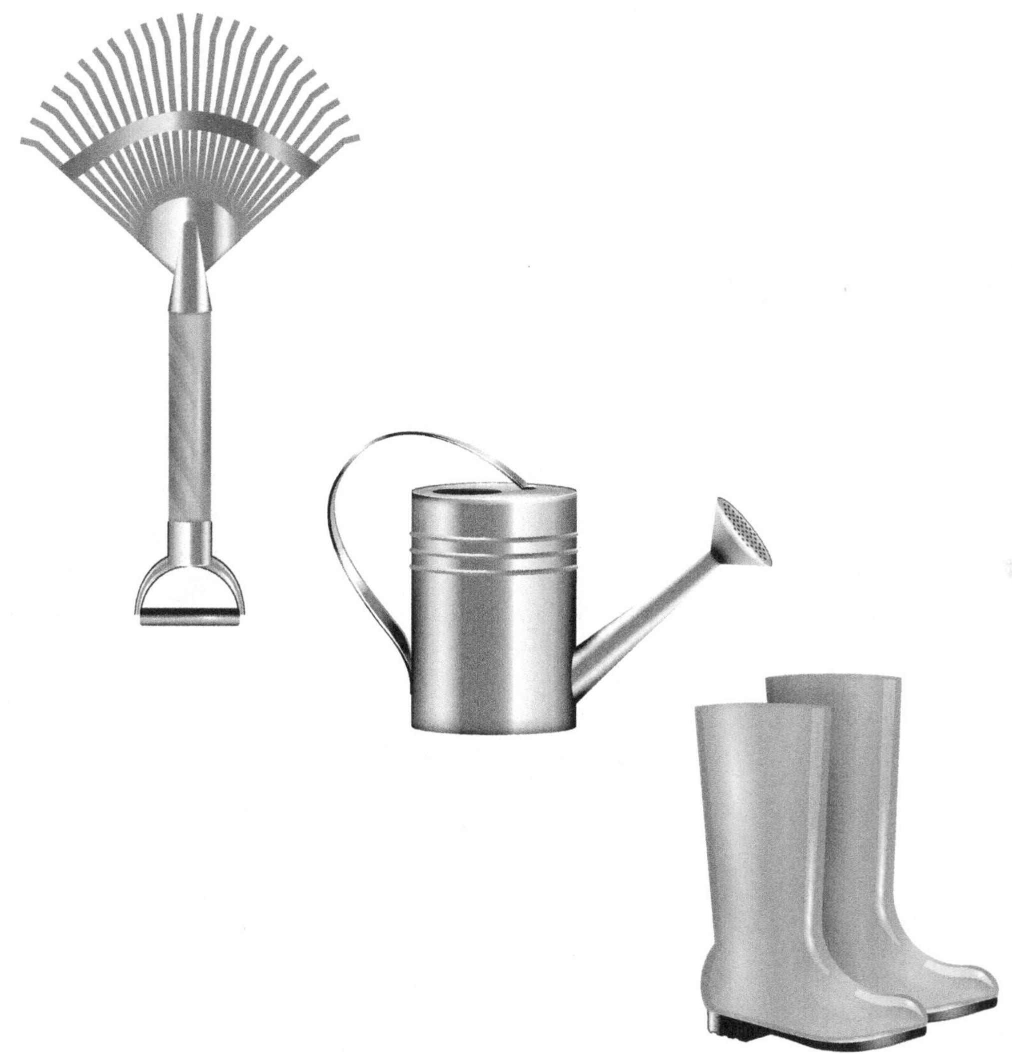

Turn the page to continue

This puzzle is continued from the previous page.

PARTICULAR PICTURES..... CONTINUED

Did you study the three items on the previous page? Great! Now pick out the three items that you tried to memorize.

Solution on page 136

Lovely Lists... Gardening

In these puzzles, the goal is to memorize the list, and then turn the page and circle the words you remember in the word grid.

Derek needs to go shopping before he works on his garden. He has a list of items he wants to buy. Once you think you've memorized his list turn the page.

Derek's List

shovel	hoe
fertilizer	basket
planter	rocks

turn the page to continue

Susan needs to go shopping before she works on her garden. She has a list of items she wants to buy. Once you think you've memorized her list turn the page.

Susan's List

twine	gloves
mulch	saw
rake	flowers

turn the page to continue

These two puzzles are continued from the previous page.

Derek's List

Circle the items that you remember from Derek's list in the word grid to the right.

seeds	sand	hoe
shovel	tree	shoes
bench	fertilizer	can
paint	bags	bucket
basket	ribbon	lights
mower	clipper	planter
rocks	moss	bulbs

◇◇

Susan's List

Circle the items that you remember from Susan's list in the word grid to the right.

gloves	herbs	soil
planks	nails	saw
rake	hose	fork
bin	mulch	flowers
boots	broom	wire
twine	spade	ladder
seedlings	tray	shears

Solution on page 136

Delightful Details

Take a look at the picture below. On the next page is an identical picture that is missing two details. When you are ready, turn the page and fill in the two missing detail.

LET'S GARDEN

Turn the page to continue

This puzzle is continued from the previous page.

Delightful Details... Continued

Have you looked at the picture on the previous page? Great! Now draw in the two details that will make the image below identical to the image on the previous page.

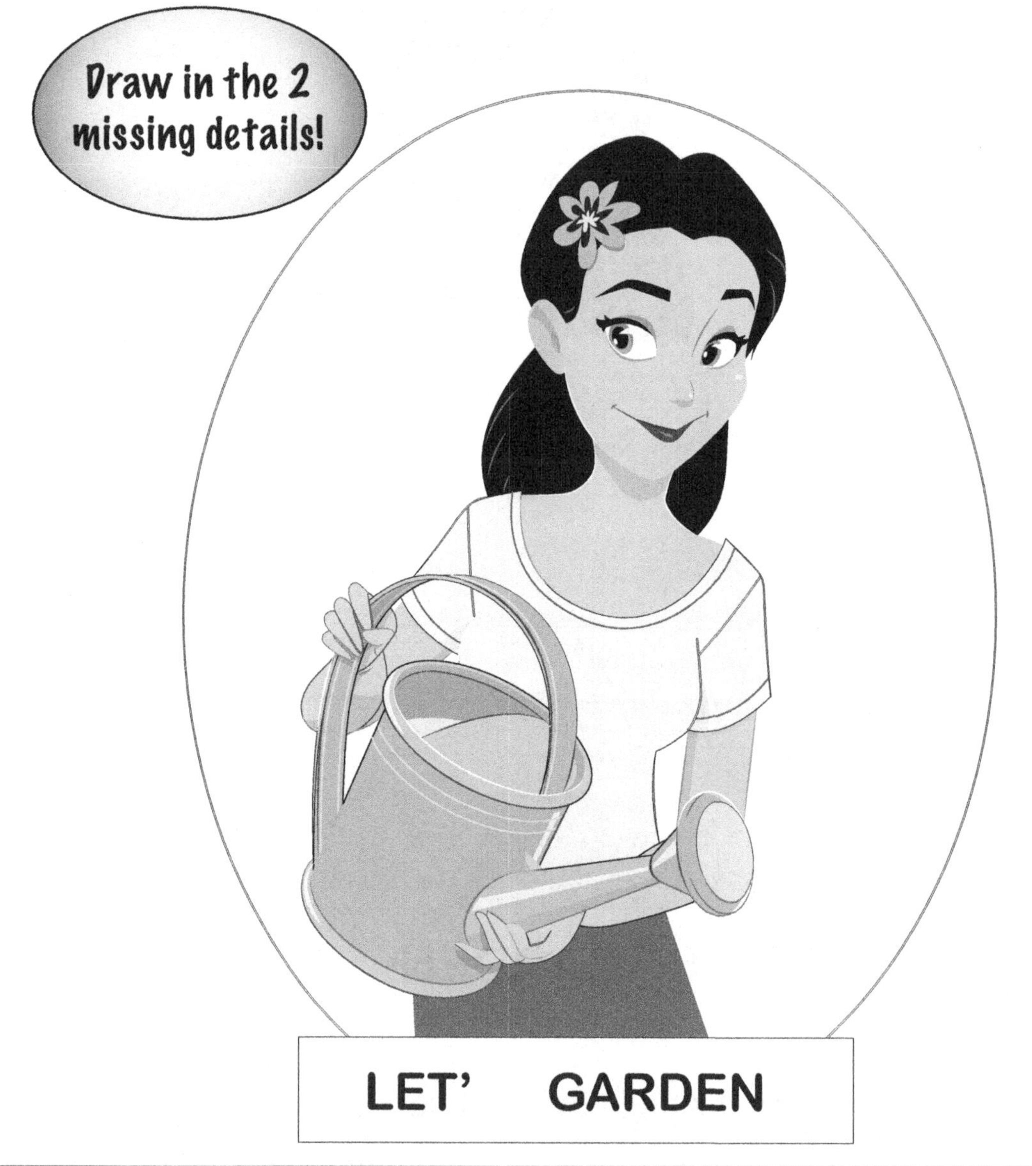
Draw in the 2 missing details!
LET' GARDEN

Solution on page 136

Cool Categories!

Make a list of the names of different flowers. How many can you name?

1. ______
2. ______
3. ______
4. ______
5. ______
6. ______
7. ______
8. ______
9. ______
10. ______
11. ______
12. ______
13 ______
14. ______
15. ______
16. ______
17. ______
18. ______
19. ______
20. ______
21. ______
22. ______

Make a list of the names of different trees. How many can you name?

1. ______
2. ______
3. ______
4. ______
5. ______
6. ______
7. ______
8. ______
9. ______
10. ______
11. ______
12. ______
13 ______
14. ______
15. ______
16. ______
17. ______
18. ______
19. ______
20. ______
21. ______
22. ______

Solution on page 136

SUDOKU

In this sudoku puzzle, use the numbers 1 to 9 to fill in the grid. To complete the grid, you need follow three rules:

1. Every vertical row has the numbers 1, 2, 3, 4, 5, 6, 7, 8 and 9 only once.
2. Every horizontal row has the numbers 1, 2, 3, 4, 5, 6, 7, 8 and 9 only once.
3. Each 3 by 3 square has the numbers 1, 2, 3, 4, 5, 6, 7, 8 and 9 only once.

	4	9	7	5			6	8
5	6	8	9		1	7		3
2		1	6	8	3	9	4	5
4	1	5		7	9	8	3	6
8	3		4	1	6		7	9
	9	7	8	3		4	1	
9		3	1	6	4	2	5	7
1	2		5		7	3		4
7	5	4		2	8	6	9	

Solution on page 137

BACKWARDS SDRAWKCAB

In this activity, the goal is to write out the sentence backwards. Try to minimize the number of times you look at the original sentence to increase the level of difficulty of this memory challenge.

1. Everything is coming up roses.

Write it backwards: ________________________________

2. April showers bring May flowers.

Write it backwards: ________________________________

3. You reap what you sow.

Write it backwards: ________________________________

4. The tree is known by its fruit.

Write it backwards: ________________________________

Solution on page 137

Writing about your life...

Describe your favorite garden. Was it one you had at your home? Or a garden you visited? What plants were there?

WORD SEARCH...

LANDSCAPING

Find the words below in the letter grid. Words may be hidden in an across, down, or diagonal direction. Also, the words may be spelled forwards or backwards.

Word List:

GRASS	CONCRETE	TRELLIS
BUSHES	PATIO	TREES
GAZEBO	TWIGS	FENCE
POND	DECK	SAND
SOIL	PLANTER	BENCH

J	D	B	U	S	H	E	S	Y	C	G	S	K	C	E	D
T	L	I	O	S	Z	X	V	T	S	G	I	W	T	E	R
E	T	G	P	A	L	A	I	R	E	T	N	A	L	P	K
T	R	E	L	L	I	S	U	E	T	E	R	C	N	O	C
T	C	W	G	H	Y	N	E	N	S	Y	Y	C	S	B	O
G	W	Y	C	C	H	S	S	A	N	D	Z	S	F	E	I
N	W	N	I	F	E	N	C	E	G	P	A	C	X	Z	T
R	E	J	C	F	D	N	O	P	G	R	Q	N	S	A	A
B	U	F	T	R	E	E	S	Y	G	C	O	G	W	G	P

Solution on page 137

SPOT THE ODD ONE OUT

Find the picture that is different from the rest.

Solution on page 138

The Memory Challenge

This activity is the hardest of the short-term memory games. Below is a list of seven random words. The goal is to memorize the words, then turn the page, and write the words out in order.

The List:

1. Violin
2. Bed
3. Window
4. Cookie
5. Bench
6. Rose
7. Book
8. Plate

A HINT... (or how to make this challenge doable)

To help memorize a list of unrelated items, you can use your imagination to make the items more memorable.

For example, if you were trying to remember the list:

A. Rabbit
B. Balloon
C. Spoon

You could imagine..... A rabbit (Item A) hopping along. The rabbit spots a balloon (Item B), and starts chasing the it. When the rabbit catches up to the balloon, the balloon pops, and a giant spoon (Item C) appears!

Consider trying this approach with the list to the left.

Turn the page when you have memorized the items.

Short-Term Memory

This puzzle is continued from the previous page.

The Memory Challenge Continued

Write the eight items you memorized from the previous page in the spaces provided.

1. ____________________
2. ____________________
3. ____________________
4. ____________________
5. ____________________
6. ____________________
7. ____________________
8. ____________________

Brain Game

Well Made Words

Create words out of the letters provided. You can use each letter only once per word.

Letters

U A D S Y T

Words

____________________ ____________________

____________________ ____________________

____________________ ____________________

____________________ ____________________

____________________ ____________________

____________________ ____________________

____________________ ____________________

Solution on page 138

Section Four

Memory Activities, Puzzles, and Brain Games

Cards & Other Games

Includes Delightful Details, Rhyme Time, Cool Categories, Particular Pictures, Writing About Your Life, Spot the Odd One Out, Backwards, Crossword, Word Search, Sudoku and The Memory Challenge

RHYME TIME

In this activity, the goal is to write down words that rhyme with the specific "given" word. Take some time to think of as many words as you can.

List words that rhyme with "GAME"

List words that rhyme with "DICE"

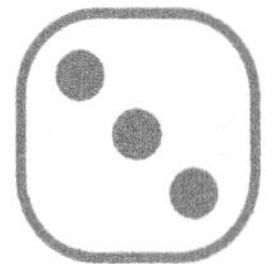
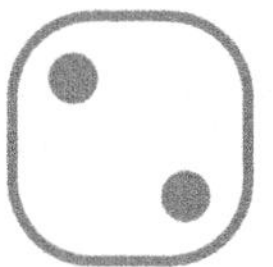

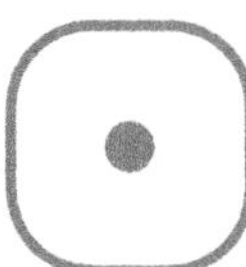

Solution on page 138

PARTICULAR PICTURES

Take a look at the three cards below. Take your time to memorize the three cards. Then turn the page and pick out the three cards that you memorized.

Turn the page to continue

This puzzle is continued from the previous page.

PARTICULAR PICTURES.... CONTINUED

Did you study the three cards on the previous page? Great! Now circle the three cards that you tried to memorize.

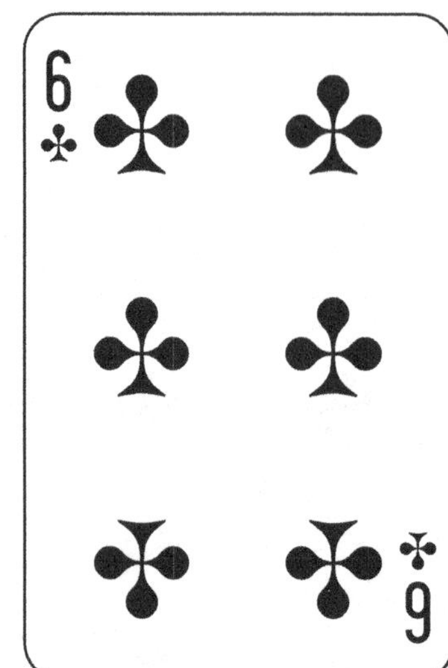

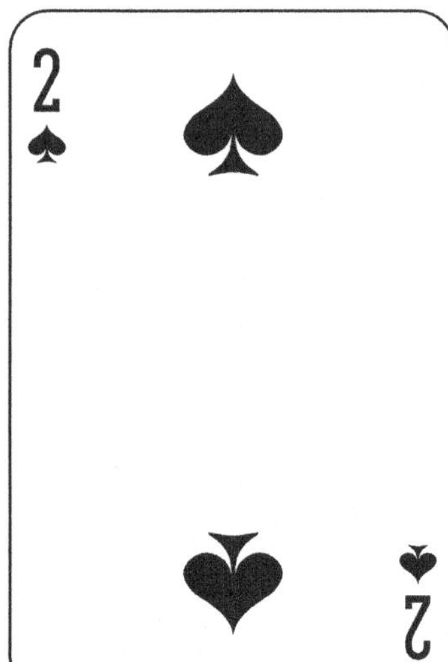

Solution on page 139

Lots of Numbers

Take some time to memorize Jim's favorite numbers which he uses to play the lottery. Then turn the page and circle the numbers you remember in the number grid.

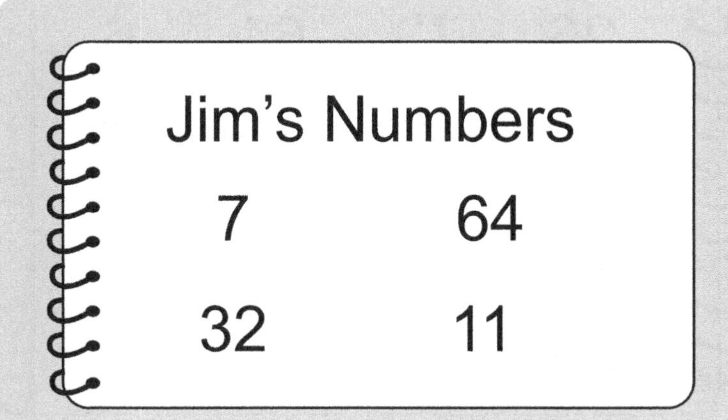

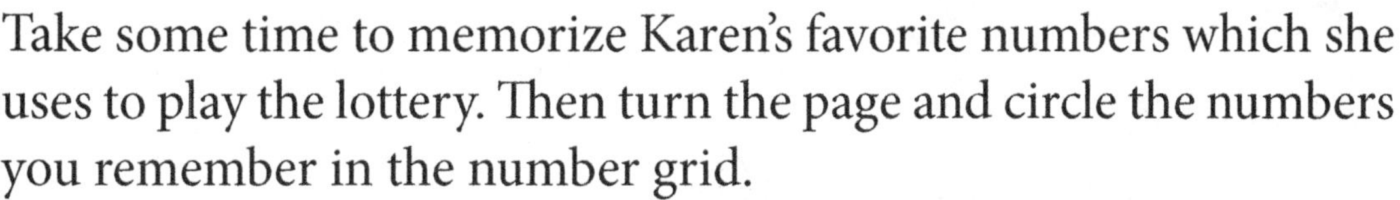

Take some time to memorize Karen's favorite numbers which she uses to play the lottery. Then turn the page and circle the numbers you remember in the number grid.

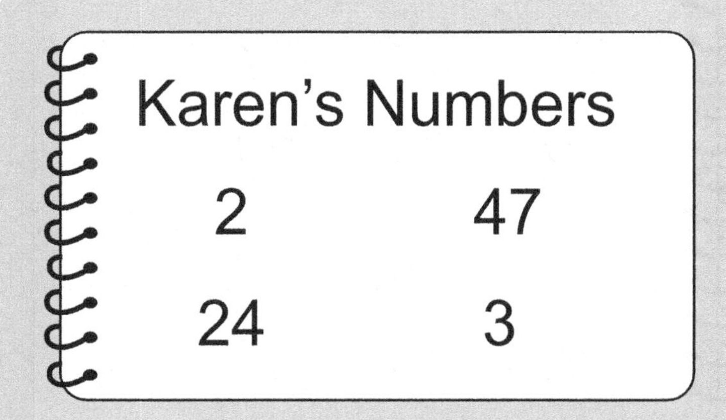

These two puzzles are continued from the previous page.

Jim's Numbers

Have you looked at Jim's number list from the previous page? Now try to circle each number you remember in the number grid.

9	81	2	11
7	5	71	9
26	73	64	6
55	1	72	83
76	32	4	42
58	14	6	3

Karen's Numbers

Have you looked at Karen's number list from the previous page? Now try to circle each number you remember in the number grid.

90	2	65	3
68	7	62	5
51	27	47	86
72	54	98	4
24	16	18	93
76	45	4	3

Solution on page 139

Delightful Details

1. Take a look at the picture to the right. On the next page is an identical picture, that is missing one detail. When you are ready, turn the page and fill in the missing detail.

Turn the page to continue

2. Take a look at the picture to the right. On the next page is an identical picture, that is missing one detail. When you are ready, turn the page and fill in the missing detail.

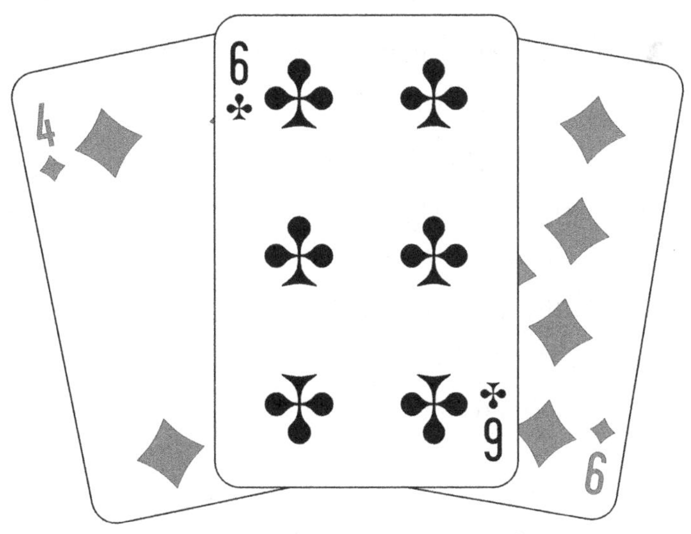

Turn the page to continue

These two puzzles are continued from the previous page.

1. Have you studied the picture on the previous page? Great! Now draw in the one detail that will make the image to the right, identical to the image on the previous page.

Draw in the 1 missing detail!

From the previous page

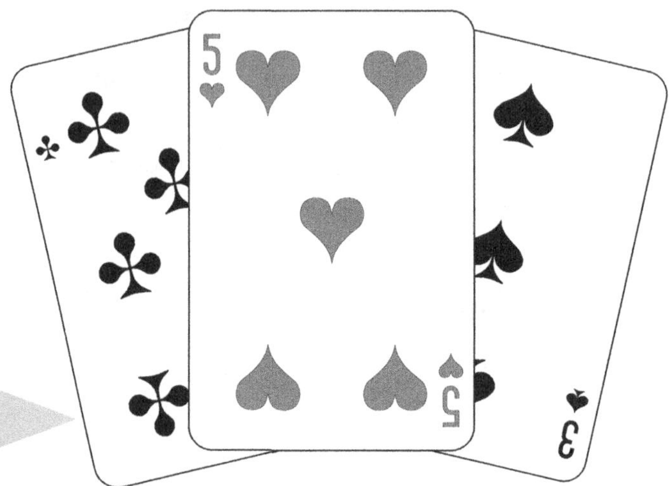

2. Have you studied the picture on the previous page? Great! Now draw in the one detail that will make the image to the right, identical to the image on the previous page.

Draw in the 1 missing detail!

From the previous page

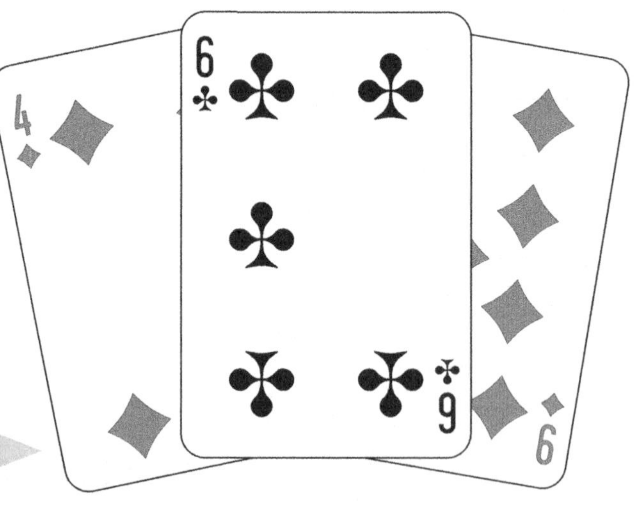

Solution on page 139

Cool Categories!

Make a list of different card games. How many can you name?

1. ________
2. ________
3. ________
4. ________
5. ________
6. ________
7. ________
8. ________
9. ________
10. ________
11. ________
12. ________

13 ________

14. ________
15. ________
16. ________
17. ________
18. ________
19. ________
20. ________
21. ________
22. ________

Make a list of different board games. How many can you name?

1. ________
2. ________
3. ________
4. ________
5. ________
6. ________
7. ________
8. ________
9. ________
10. ________
11. ________
12. ________

13 ________

14. ________
15. ________
16. ________
17. ________
18. ________
19. ________
20. ________
21. ________
22. ________

Solution on page 140

CROSSWORD

In this puzzle, write the answer to each clue in the crossword grid. One letter goes into each square.

ACROSS

1) Piece to capture to win in chess
3) 'Set _____ to paper'
4) 'Play your ________ right'
7) Game where one person is 'it'
8) A yellow fruit
10) 'From _____ to shining sea'
11) Opposite of bottom
12) 'You can't _____ it with you'
15) Pull gently
16) Baseball _____, on one's head
18) Round cooking containers
19) Poetry set to music
21) Back of the neck
22) Baby dog
24) Heavy cord
26) Opposite of on
27) Look forward to doing something
29) Go into a room
31) Holds coffee
32) Messy person
33) Often start of a letter
34) ______ photography, take photos from the sky
35) A sojourn away from home
36) Pastry shell

DOWN

1) 'Go fly a _______!'
2) 'Ships passing in the ______.'
3) Earth or Saturn
4) Put it on when its cold
5) Give deference to
6) Moved in water
9) Letters from one word rearranged to make a new word
13) Response to a question
14) A belief
17) Amuse oneself
20) Salt's partner
23) 'A square ____ in a round hole'
25) Get ready
28) Long-eared animal
30) Exhausted
31) Yield of a farm
32) Narrow opening
33) Round mark

1 2 3 4 5 6 7 8 9 10 11 12 13 14 15 16 17 18 19 20 21 22 23 24 25 26 27 28 29 30 31 32 33 34 35 36

Solution on page 140

SUDOKU

In this sudoku puzzle, use the numbers 1 to 9 to fill in the grid. To complete the grid, you need follow three rules:

1. Every vertical row has the numbers 1, 2, 3, 4, 5, 6, 7, 8 and 9 only once.
2. Every horizontal row has the numbers 1, 2, 3, 4, 5, 6, 7, 8 and 9 only once.
3. Each 3 by 3 square has the numbers 1, 2, 3, 4, 5, 6, 7, 8 and 9 only once.

2	6	7		1	5	3	9	8
	8	1	7		3		5	4
5	3		8	9		6	1	
1		3	2		6	4	7	9
4	9	6		7	1	8		2
7		8	9	3	4	1		5
3	7		1	4	9	5	8	
	4	9	3		8	7		1
8	1	5		2	7		4	3

Solution on page 140

BACKWARDS SDRAWKCAB

In this activity, the goal is to write out the sentence backwards. Try to minimize the number of times you look at the original sentence to increase the level of difficulty of this memory challenge.

1. Keep your cards close to your chest.

Write it backwards: ______________________________

2. Beat someone at their own game.

Write it backwards: ______________________________

3. Time flies when your having fun.

Write it backwards: ______________________________

4. More fun than a barrel of monkeys.

Write it backwards: ______________________________

Solution on page 141

Writing about your life...

Describe your favorite card game or board game. Why is it your favorite? When did you first play your favorite game?

WORD SEARCH...

FUN & GAMES

Find the words below in the letter grid. Words may be hidden in an across, down, or diagonal direction. Also, the words may be spelled forwards or backwards.

Word List:

COMPETE	TURN	SPEED
STRATEGY	PLAYER	JOIN
ENJOY	DICE	RULES
REWARD	TRICKY	SKILLS
BET	WIN	CHANCE

V	E	C	I	D	T	E	B	V	K	E	R	X	W	B	S
N	Y	G	E	T	A	R	T	S	Z	D	C	B	Y	K	P
T	O	X	E	D	U	E	W	R	R	U	U	N	I	Q	I
J	C	T	B	K	T	Y	B	A	B	J	S	L	A	O	N
O	M	J	I	E	K	D	W	H	N	A	L	T	W	H	B
I	O	Z	P	C	V	E	S	E	P	S	C	A	X	V	C
N	V	M	I	Q	R	E	X	K	P	N	Y	O	J	N	E
W	O	R	N	X	L	P	G	R	I	R	E	Y	A	L	P
C	T	R	U	L	E	S	G	W	W	T	U	R	N	F	V

Solution on page 141

SPOT THE ODD ONE OUT

Find the picture that is different from the rest.

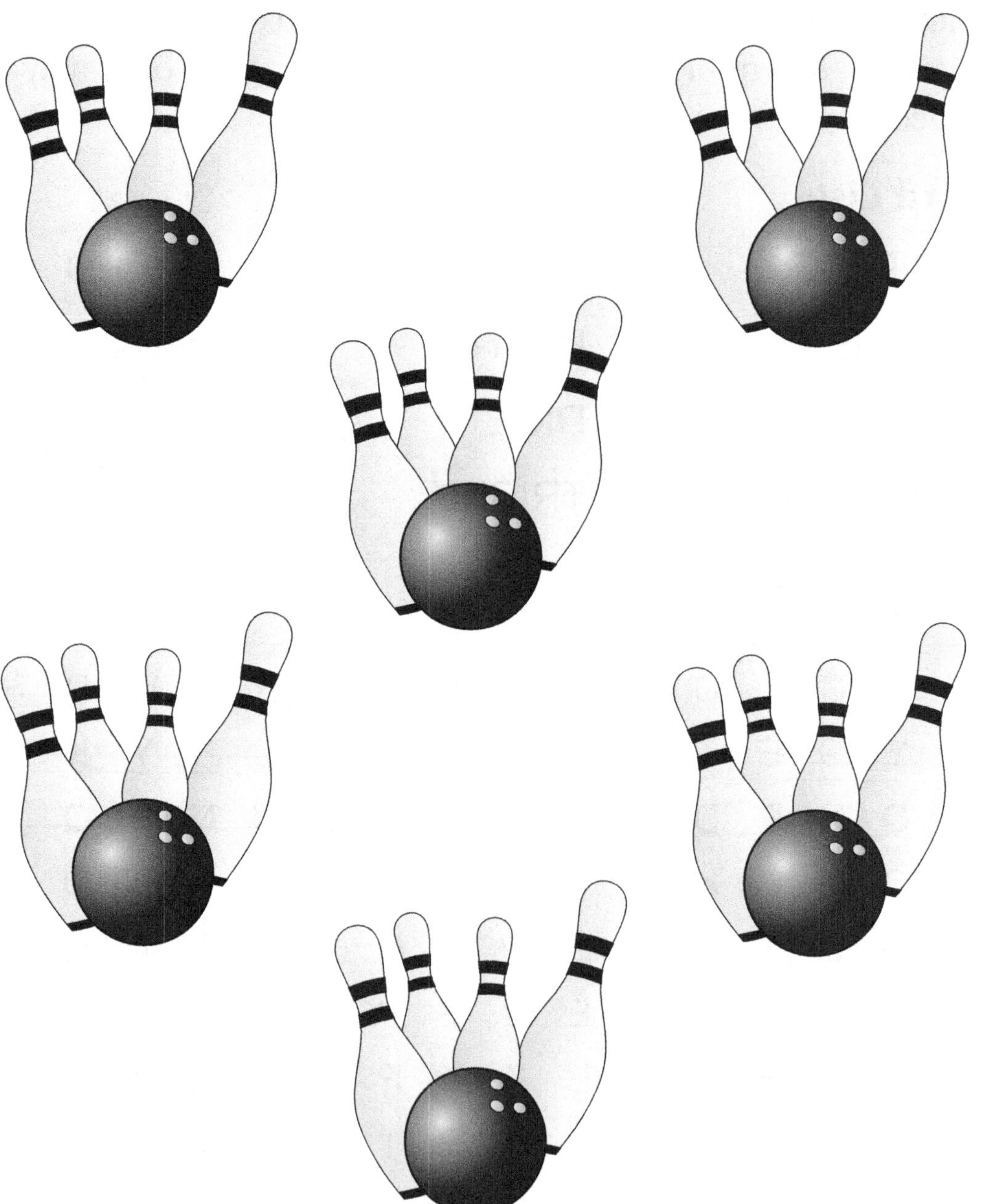

Solution on page 141

The Memory Challenge

This activity is the hardest of the short-term memory games. Below is a list of seven random words. The goal is to memorize the words, then turn the page, and write the words out in order.

The List:

1. Purse
2. Kangaroo
3. Jam
4. Cup
5. Fence
6. Paper
7. Leaf
8. Stream

A HINT... (or how to make this challenge doable)

To help memorize a list of unrelated items, you can use your imagination to make the items more memorable.

For example, if you were trying to remember the list:

A. Rabbit
B. Balloon
C. Spoon

You could imagine..... A rabbit (Item A) hopping along. The rabbit spots a balloon (Item B), and starts chasing the it. When the rabbit catches up to the balloon, the balloon pops, and a giant spoon (Item C) appears!

Consider trying this approach with the list to the left.

Turn the page when you have memorized the items.

This puzzle is continued from the previous page.

The Memory Challenge Continued

Write the eight items you memorized from the previous page in the spaces provided.

1. ____________________ 5. ____________________

2. ____________________ 6. ____________________

3. ____________________ 7. ____________________

4. ____________________ 8. ____________________

Brain Game

Well Made Words

Create words out of the letters provided. You can use each letter only once per word.

Letters

A C G T R E

Words

Solution on page 142

Section Five

Memory Activities, Puzzles, and Brain Games

Lovely Vacations

Includes Delightful Details, Rhyme Time, Cool Categories, Particular Pictures, Writing About Your Life, Spot the Odd One Out, Backwards, Word Search, Sudoku, and The Memory Challenge

RHYME TIME

In this activity, the goal is to write down words that rhyme with the specific "given" word. Take some time to think of as many words as you can.

List items that rhyme with "TRIP"

_______________ _______________ _______________
_______________ _______________ _______________
_______________ _______________ _______________
_______________ _______________ _______________
_______________ _______________ _______________

List items that rhyme with "FUN"

_______________ _______________ _______________
_______________ _______________ _______________
_______________ _______________ _______________
_______________ _______________ _______________
_______________ _______________ _______________

Solution on page 142

PARTICULAR PICTURES

Take a look at the three pictures below. Take your time to memorize the three items. Then turn the page and pick out the three items that you memorized.

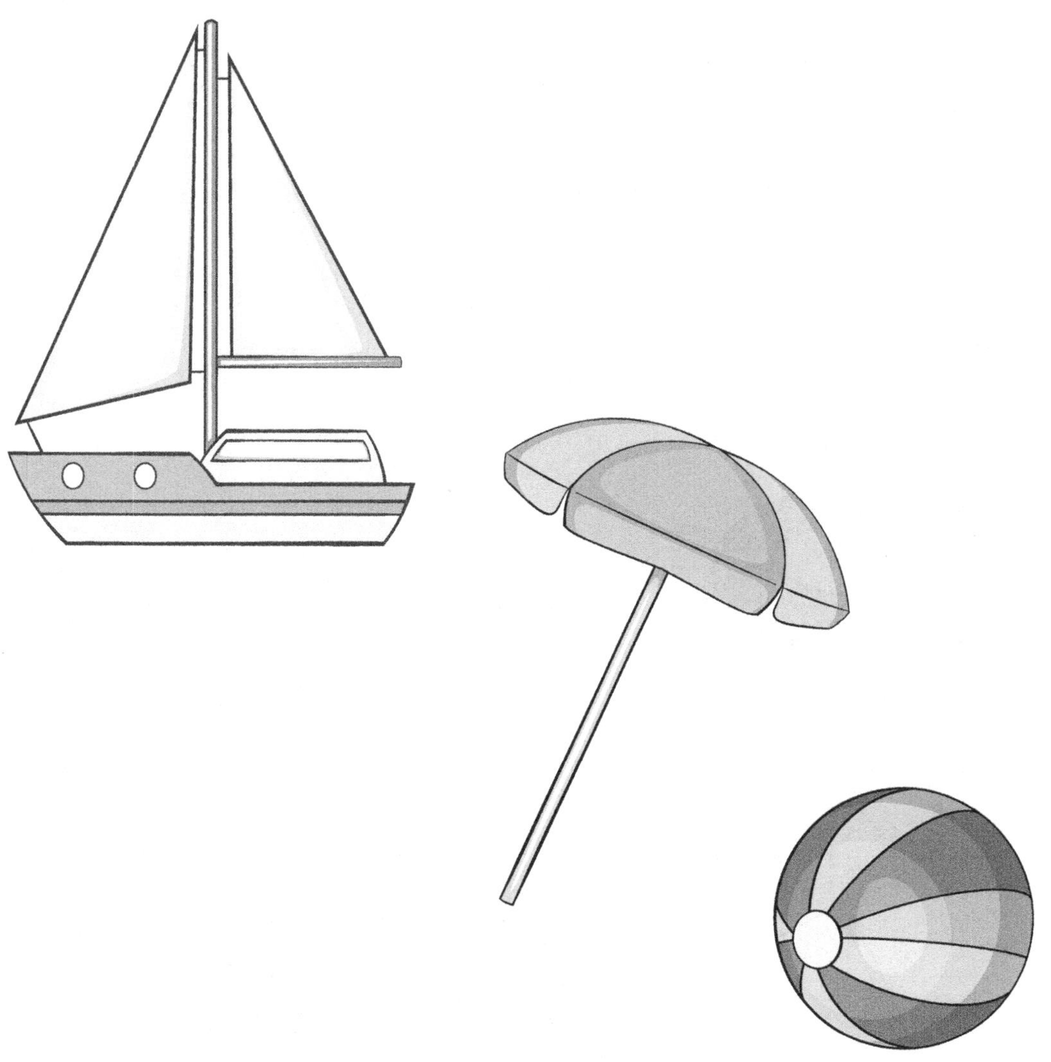

Turn the page to continue

This puzzle is continued from the previous page.

PARTICULAR PICTURES..... CONTINUED

Did you study the three items on the previous page? Great! Now pick out the three items that you tried to memorize.

Solution on page 142

Lovely Lists..... Packing

In these puzzles, the goal is to memorize the list, and then turn the page and circle the words you remember in the word grid.

Ray needs to go shopping for his upcoming vacation. To the right is a list of items he wants to buy for the trip. Once you think you've memorized his list turn the page.

Ray's List

socks	camera
lotion	shoes
hat	map

Turn the page

Kim needs to go shopping for her upcoming vacation. To the right is a list of items she wants to buy for the trip. Once you think you've memorized her list turn the page.

Kim's List

shorts	blanket
journal	tent
bag	rope

Turn the page

These two puzzles are continued from the previous page.

Ray's List

Circle the items that you remember from Ray's list in the word grid to the right.

pants	soap	shampoo
socks	boots	lotion
pen	paper	book
hat	pencil	camera
vest	shoes	coat
map	candy	sweater
curtain	tissues	t-shirt

◇◇

Kim's List

Circle the items that you remember from Kim's list in the word grid to the right.

rope	dress	journal
shorts	skirt	sandals
purse	watch	lamp
matches	canoe	blanket
bag	kayak	jacket
net	tent	mat
pan	plate	forks

Solution on page 143

Delightful Details

Take a look at the picture below. On the next page, is an identical picture, that is missing two details. When you are ready, turn the page and fill in the two missing details.

Turn the page to continue

This puzzle is continued from the previous page.

Delightful Details..... Continued

Have you looked at the picture on the previous page? Great! Now draw in the two details, that will make the image below, identical to the image on the previous page.

Draw in the 2 missing details!

Solution on page 143

Cool Categories!

Make a list of capital cities from around the world. How many can you name?

1.
2.
3.
4.
5.
6.
7.
8.
9.
10.
11.
12.
13
14.
15.
16.
17.
18.
19.
20.
21.
22.

Make a list of famous landmarks. How many can you name?

1.
2.
3.
4.
5.
6.
7.
8.
9.
10.
11.
12.
13
14.
15.
16.
17.
18.
19.
20.
21.
22.

Solution on page 143

SUDOKU

In this sudoku puzzle, use the numbers 1 to 9 to fill in the grid. To complete the grid, you need follow three rules:

1. Every vertical row has the numbers 1, 2, 3, 4, 5, 6, 7, 8 and 9 only once.
2. Every horizontal row has the numbers 1, 2, 3, 4, 5, 6, 7, 8 and 9 only once.
3. Each 3 by 3 square has the numbers 1, 2, 3, 4, 5, 6, 7, 8 and 9 only once.

8	7	9	4	1		3		6
	1	4		3	8	7	9	2
5		3	6	9	7		8	1
9	4	1	8		3	2		5
	5		9	2	4	6	1	
2	8	6		7	5	9	4	3
1		2	7	8		5	6	
4	9	8		5	6	1		7
	6	5	2		1		3	9

Solution on page 144

BACKWARDS SDRAWKCAB

In this activity, the goal is to write out the sentence backwards. Try to minimize the number of times you look at the original sentence to increase the level of difficulty of this memory challenge.

1. Travel broadens the mind.

Write it backwards: ______________________________

2. Off the beaten track.

Write it backwards: ______________________________

3. From sea to shining sea.

Write it backwards: ______________________________

4. Live out of a suitcase.

Write it backwards: ______________________________

Solution on page 144

Writing about your life...

Describe one of your favorite trips or vacations. Why was it your favorite? Where did you go? And what did you do?

WORD SEARCH...
SKI TRIP

Find the words below in the letter grid. Words may be hidden in an across, down, or diagonal direction. Also, the words may be spelled forwards or backwards.

Word List:

DOWNHILL	MOGULS	SKIS
SLOPES	LODGE	BOOTS
ICE	GLOVES	JACKET
POLES	GOGGLES	LIFT
HELMET	FREESTYLE	SNOW

E	X	S	E	P	O	L	S	B	S	E	L	G	G	O	G
L	S	B	T	H	K	W	O	P	C	Q	L	W	X	N	Z
Y	E	O	S	F	B	M	O	G	U	L	S	D	E	C	I
T	L	O	K	D	I	Z	O	T	I	S	Y	W	T	O	E
S	O	T	I	L	V	L	E	H	E	E	Y	O	E	I	X
E	P	S	S	L	X	M	N	V	U	G	I	N	K	C	R
E	W	L	G	B	L	W	O	R	Z	D	U	S	C	F	W
R	J	A	L	E	O	L	L	Z	Z	O	W	V	A	Q	P
F	O	G	H	D	G	P	H	F	G	L	K	E	J	Z	F

Solution on page 144

SPOT THE ODD ONE OUT

Find the picture that is different from the rest.

Solution on page 145

The Memory Challenge

This activity is the hardest of the short-term memory games. Below is a list of seven random words. The goal is to memorize the words in order, then turn the page, and write the words down.

The List:

1. Racket
2. Grass
3. Dress
4. Car
5. Scarf
6. Banana
7. Bowl
8. Bear

A HINT... (or how to make this challenge doable)

To help memorize a list of unrelated items, you can use your imagination to make the items more memorable.

For example, if you were trying to remember the list:

A. Rabbit
B. Balloon
C. Spoon

You could imagine..... A rabbit (Item A) hopping along. The rabbit spots a balloon (Item B), and starts chasing the it. When the rabbit catches up to the balloon, the balloon pops, and a giant spoon (Item C) appears!

Consider trying this approach with the list to the left.

Turn the page when you have memorized the items.

This puzzle is continued from the previous page.

The Memory Challenge Continued

Write the eight items you memorized from the previous page in the spaces provided.

1. ______________________
2. ______________________
3. ______________________
4. ______________________
5. ______________________
6. ______________________
7. ______________________
8. ______________________

Brain Game

Well Made Words

Create words out of the letters provided. You can use each letter only once per word.

Letters	Words	
F R B A Y I	______________	______________
	______________	______________
	______________	______________
	______________	______________
	______________	______________
	______________	______________
	______________	______________

Solution on page 145

Section Six

Memory Activities, Puzzles, and Brain Games

Art & Artists

Includes Delightful Details, Rhyme Time, Cool Categories, Particular Pictures, Writing About Your Life, Spot the Odd One Out, Backwards, Word Search, Sudoku, and The Memory Challenge

RHYME TIME

In this activity, the goal is to write down words that rhyme with the specific "given" word. Take some time to think of as many words as you can.

List items that rhyme "BRUSH"

______	______	______
______	______	______
______	______	______
______	______	______
______	______	______

List items that rhyme with "DRAW"

______	______	______
______	______	______
______	______	______
______	______	______
______	______	______

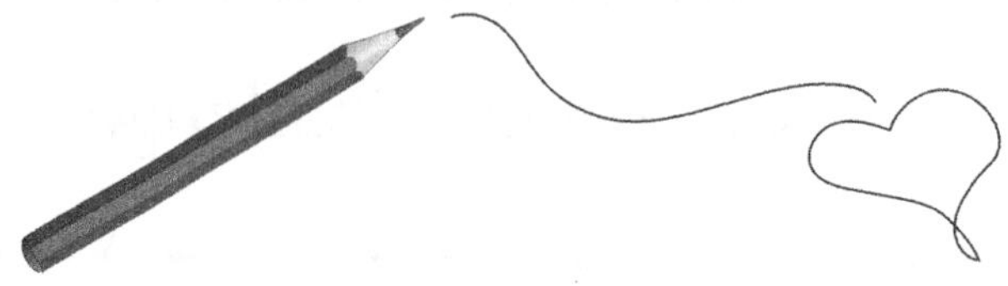

Solution on page 145

PARTICULAR PICTURES

Take a look at the three pictures below. Take your time to memorize the three items. Then turn the page and pick out the three items that you memorized.

Turn the page to continue

This puzzle is continued from the previous page.

PARTICULAR PICTURES..... CONTINUED

Did you study the three items on the previous page? Great! Now pick out the three items that you tried to memorize.

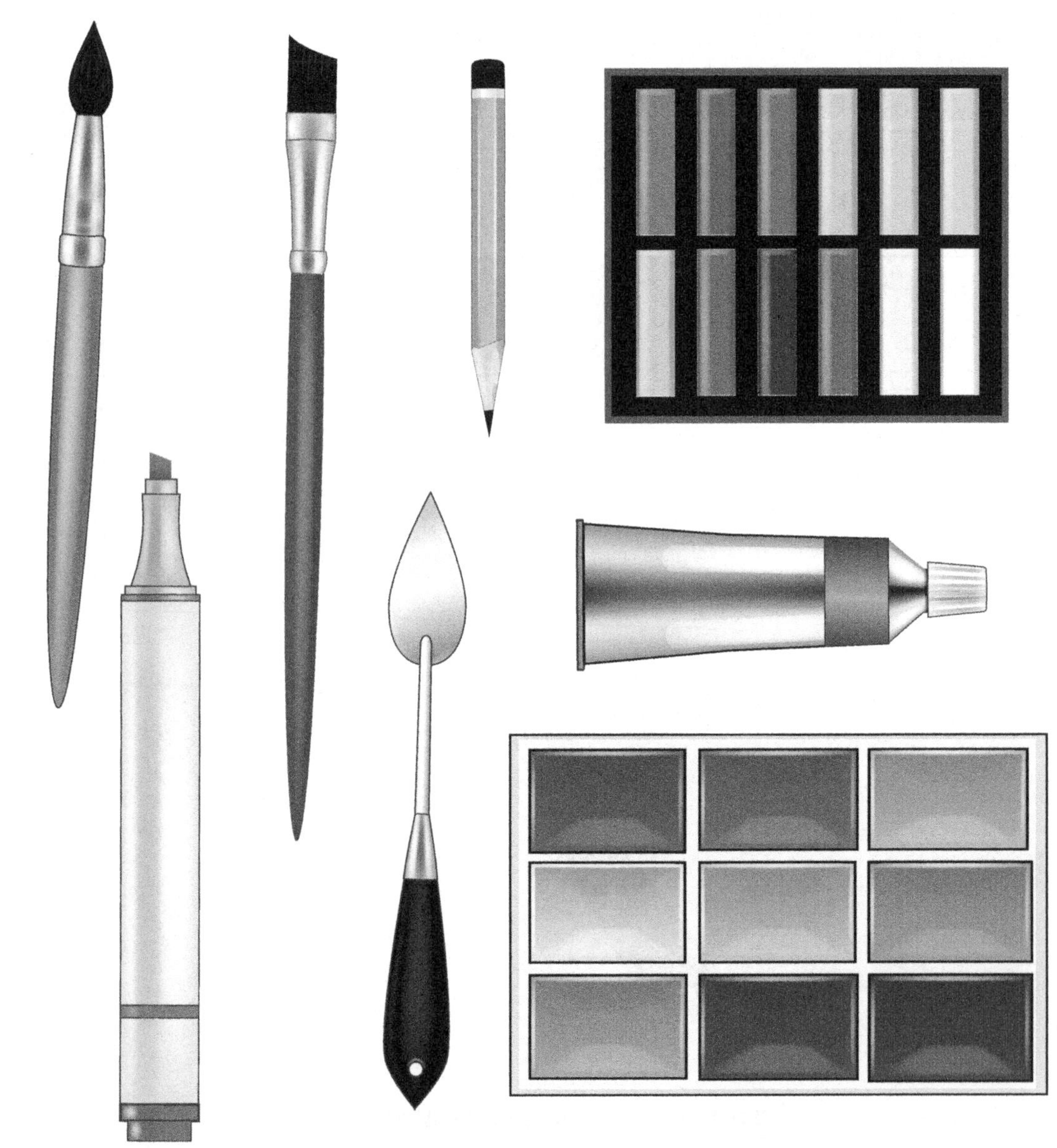

Solution on page 145

Lovely Lists... Supplies

In these puzzles, the goal is to memorize the list, and then turn the page and circle the words you remember in the word grid.

Cory is going shopping for his new art project. To the right is a list of items he wants to buy, so he can get started. Once you think you've memorized his list turn the page.

Cory's List

glue
brushes
primer
pastels
paper
ink

turn the page to continue

◇◇

Trudie is going shopping for her new art project. To the right is a list of items she wants to buy so she can get started. Once you think you've memorized her list turn the page.

Trudie's List

clay
glaze
mallet
sponge
marker
mold

turn the page to continue

These two puzzles are continued from the previous page.

Cory's List

Circle the items that you remember from Cory's list in the word grid to the right.

chalk	glue	pencil
brushes	paint	graphite
paste	cutter	primer
knife	pastels	scissors
canvas	pallet	tray
paper	camera	printer
stamp	bowl	ink

◇◇

Trudie's List

Circle the items that you remember from Trudie's list in the word grid to the right.

sponge	pick	shaper
tongs	marker	pins
mold	kiln	blanket
mallet	wire	scraper
gloves	staples	sealer
wheel	glaze	mats
plaster	tiles	clay

Solution on page 146

Delightful Details

Take a look at the picture below. On the next page is an identical picture that is missing two details. When you are ready, turn the page and fill in the two missing detail.

Turn the page to continue

This puzzle is continued from the previous page.

Delightful Details..... Continued

Have you looked at the picture on the previous page? Great! Now draw in the two details that will make the image below identical to the image on the previous page.

Draw in the 2 missing details!

Solution on page 146

Cool Categories!

Make a list of famous artists. How many artists can you name?

1. __________
2. __________
3. __________
4. __________
5. __________
6. __________
7. __________
8. __________
9. __________
10. __________
11. __________
12. __________
13 __________
14. __________
15. __________
16. __________
17. __________
18. __________
19. __________
20. __________
21. __________
22. __________

Make a list of different art galleries or museums. How many can you name?

1. __________
2. __________
3. __________
4. __________
5. __________
6. __________
7. __________
8. __________
9. __________
10. __________
11. __________
12. __________
13 __________
14. __________
15. __________
16. __________
17. __________
18. __________
19. __________
20. __________
21. __________
22. __________

Solution on page 146

SUDOKU

In this sudoku puzzle, use the numbers 1 to 9 to fill in the grid. To complete the grid, you need follow three rules:

1. Every vertical row has the numbers 1, 2, 3, 4, 5, 6, 7, 8 and 9 only once.
2. Every horizontal row has the numbers 1, 2, 3, 4, 5, 6, 7, 8 and 9 only once.
3. Each 3 by 3 square has the numbers 1, 2, 3, 4, 5, 6, 7, 8 and 9 only once.

1		3	4		2	5	6	8
2	7	8	5	6		4	9	
	6	5		9	3		1	7
7	2	6	1	5		3	8	4
8		9		3	6	1		5
3	5		7		8	9	2	
	3	2	6	1		8	4	9
6	8		9		5		3	1
9		7	3	8	4	6		2

Solution on page 147

BACKWARDS SDRAWKCAB

In this activity, the goal is to write out the sentence backwards. Try to minimize the number of times you look at the original sentence to increase the level of difficulty of this memory challenge.

1. A picture is worth a thousand words.

Write it backwards: ______________________________

2. Paint yourself into a corner.

Write it backwards: ______________________________

3. Color outside the lines.

Write it backwards: ______________________________

4. Many hands make light work.

Write it backwards: ______________________________

Solution on page 147

Writing about your life...

Describe your favorite piece of art. Was it a gift from a family member, or something you saw in a book or museum? Who created the work? And why is it, in fact, your favorite piece of art?

WORD SEARCH...

SCULPTURE

Find the words below in the letter grid. Words may be hidden in an across, down, or diagonal direction. Also, the words may be spelled forwards or backwards.

Word List:

CARVE	MOSAIC	POLISH
MOLD	WOOD	BRONZE
ETCH	PLASTER	SHAPE
FRESCO	MARBLE	GRANITE
CHISEL	CLAY	CAST

K	E	U	I	D	L	O	M	E	X	Y	U	A	P	F	T
E	P	U	F	O	T	C	Z	E	Q	F	Y	L	R	Z	N
T	A	E	F	Y	W	N	Z	W	N	T	A	E	M	L	R
C	H	T	Q	W	O	L	Y	T	O	S	S	M	O	E	E
H	S	I	N	R	E	E	V	K	T	C	I	A	S	O	M
X	F	N	B	N	V	S	H	E	O	H	S	I	L	O	P
P	L	A	V	U	R	I	R	L	L	G	B	Y	A	L	C
O	B	R	V	J	A	H	V	E	L	B	R	A	M	F	V
E	L	G	P	G	C	C	C	A	S	T	L	D	O	O	W

Solution on page 147

SPOT THE ODD ONE OUT

Find the picture that is different from the rest.

Solution on page 148

The Memory Challenge

This activity is the hardest of the short-term memory games. Below is a list of seven random words. The goal is to memorize the words, then turn the page, and write the words out in order.

The List:

1. Phone
2. Mouse
3. Basket
4. Candy
5. Sock
6. Stick
7. Rope
8. Bicycle

A HINT... (or how to make this challenge doable)

To help memorize a list of unrelated items, you can use your imagination to make the items more memorable.

For example, if you were trying to remember the list:

A. Rabbit
B. Balloon
C. Spoon

You could imagine..... A rabbit (Item A) hopping along. The rabbit spots a balloon (Item B), and starts chasing the it. When the rabbit catches up to the balloon, the balloon pops, and a giant spoon (Item C) appears!

Consider trying this approach with the list to the left.

Turn the page when you have memorized the items.

This puzzle is continued from the previous page.

The Memory Challenge Continued

Write the eight items you memorized from the previous page in the spaces provided.

1. ____________________
2. ____________________
3. ____________________
4. ____________________
5. ____________________
6. ____________________
7. ____________________
8. ____________________

Well Made Words

Create words out of the letters provided. You can use each letter only once per word.

Letters	Words	
P I R B T E	____________	____________
	____________	____________
	____________	____________
	____________	____________
	____________	____________
	____________	____________
	____________	____________

Solution on page 148

Section Seven

Memory Activities, Puzzles, and Brain Games

Bonus Activities

Crosswords, Word Searches

Find the Differences, Which Card?

Writing About Your Life

CROSSWORD

In this puzzle, write the answer to each clue in the crossword grid. One letter goes into each square.

ACROSS

1) It takes pictures
4) Animal with an extremely long neck
8) 'Be _____ the same page'
9) Additional
10) Opposite of win
11) Charity begins ___ home
12) Dark beer
13) Chickens ____ eggs
14) A hardworking insect
15) It heats the earth
16) Three plus one
17) Account of money owed
19) Can hold a camera
21) Yours and mine
23) Sent using an envelope
26) Make money
28) The present
30) Dull or boring taste
32) 'Can't _____ the sight of'
34) Taste of a lemon
35) A food reward
36) The thinking organ

DOWN

1) Animal that has a hump that stores water
2) Wed
3) Comes after July
4) 'All that glitters, is not _______'
5) Take a break or repose
6) A young horse
7) Opposite of exit
12) Month before May
14) Creative work
15) Opposite of fast
16) Important baking ingredient
18) Opposite of quieter
20) Flower that has thorns
22) Dependable
24) ___ Landers, advice columnist
25) Opposite of high
27) 'It is _______ too late to learn'
29) Mammal with webbed feet and dark fur
30) Highest quality
31) 'Let the _______ settle'
33) ___ Rather, news anchor

Solution on page 148

WORD SEARCH...

DANCING

Find the words below in the letter grid. Words may be hidden in an across, down, or diagonal direction. Also, the words may be spelled forwards or backwards.

Word List:

SALSA	SAMBA	RUMBA
DISCO	TANGO	CONGA
TAP	JIG	WALTZ
HULA	BALLET	DANCER
MOVE	STEPS	TWIST

W	A	L	T	Z	E	J	A	L	D	T	Q	A	S	D	K
S	V	H	A	B	A	L	L	E	T	Q	L	A	V	S	R
R	L	C	N	U	Z	V	N	U	U	U	L	N	G	A	U
E	R	J	G	N	M	T	K	T	H	S	T	U	Y	M	J
C	U	Q	O	U	N	S	X	A	A	I	A	L	T	B	O
N	M	K	J	B	P	Z	A	P	U	P	G	O	S	A	C
A	B	S	D	E	L	G	N	Z	G	Z	N	Z	I	I	S
D	A	S	T	S	I	A	M	O	V	E	O	W	W	Z	I
B	O	S	U	J	B	V	Y	C	I	X	C	A	T	X	D

Solution on page 149

Which Card?

Take a moment to memorize the six cards below. On the next page, the same cards appear with one card missing. When you are ready, turn the page and try to identify the missing card.

Turn the page when you have memorized the items.

Which Card?

Which one of the following three cards is the missing card in the arrangement below?

Missing Card

?

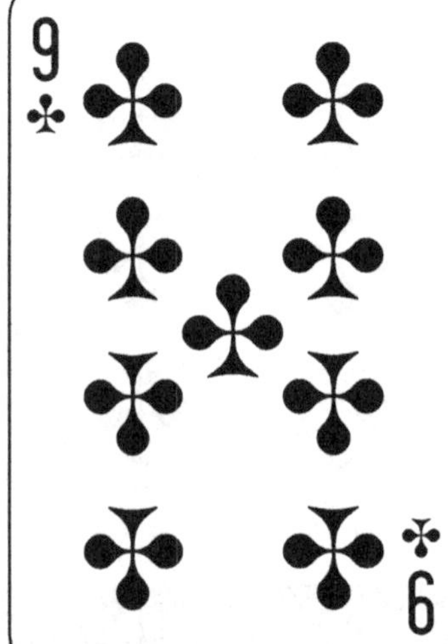

Solution on page 149

FIND THE 5 DIFFERENCES

Find the 5 difference between the two pictures.

Solution on page 149

CROSSWORD

In this puzzle, write the answer to each clue in the crossword grid. One letter goes into each square.

ACROSS

1) Smelly vegetable with layers
3) Conceal
5) Equipment used in baseball
7) What we breath
8) Kitchen tool with two arms used to serve food
9) One who doesn't tell the truth
11) Opposite of out
12) Quaint lodging
13) Makes dinner
14) '_____ it, or lose it'
16) Lets you hear
19) He customizes clothing
22) Opposite of far
24) Lease an apartment
26) Short trip to complete a task
28) 'As good as ____ gets'
29) What a chicken lays
31) 365 days
33) Opposite of outside
36) Seat for a person on a horse
37) Gave a portion to friends

DOWN

1) Marine animal with eight arms
2) Not guilty
3) Aids someone
4) Make money
5) The thinking organ
6) Reflect upon
10) Walkway in a store
15) Yes, in Spanish
17) Go faster than a walk
18) Trash
20) Change something
21) Damage something a lot
23) Have a keen interest in doing
24) Dried up grapes
25) 'My hands _____ tied'
27) 'His _____ are numbered'
30) Object of devotion
32) _______ Karenina, by Leo Tolstoy
34) Unhappy
35) Sigmund Freud's _______, ego, and super-ego

1		2			■	3			4	■	5		6
	■		■	■	■		■	■	7			■	
8					■	9		10		■		■	
	■		■	■	■		■	11		■	12		
	■	13					■		■	■		■	
14			■	■	■	■	■		■	■	■	■	■
	■		■	15	■	■	■	16		17	■	■	18
■	■	19	20				21	■	■		■	■	
■	■	■		■	■	■		■	■	22	23		
24				■	25	■		■	■	■		■	
	■	■	26					27	■	■		■	
28		■		■		■	■		■	■	29		
	■	■	■	30	■	■	■	31		32		■	
33		34				■	■		■		■	■	■
	■		■		■	■	■	■	■		■	■	35
36						■	■	37					

Solution on page 150

Classic Puzzle

WORD SEARCH...
COUNTRIES

Find the words below in the letter grid. Words may be hidden in an across, down, or diagonal direction. Also, the words may be spelled forwards or backwards.

Word List:

PERU	ITALY	GREECE
SPAIN	JAPAN	NORWAY
ENGLAND	IRELAND	BRAZIL
FRANCE	USA	CANADA
PORTUGAL	INDIA	GERMANY

H	P	O	R	T	U	G	A	L	Y	N	A	M	R	E	G
V	Z	C	I	G	R	E	E	C	E	U	W	L	T	F	I
R	N	P	A	C	A	I	D	N	I	D	Y	Q	K	R	T
Y	N	W	A	N	B	X	M	A	N	L	L	A	E	A	E
A	I	W	P	Z	A	B	X	A	Y	M	I	L	J	N	K
W	A	Z	E	J	X	D	L	L	Q	V	A	Z	A	C	A
R	P	S	R	L	A	G	A	M	V	N	G	P	A	E	T
O	S	S	U	X	N	T	C	E	D	N	A	P	Q	R	B
N	Z	M	B	E	I	A	S	U	L	J	D	C	I	M	B

Solution on page 150

Which Card?

Take a moment to memorize the six cards below. On the next page, the same cards appear with one card missing. When you are ready, turn the page and try to identify the missing card.

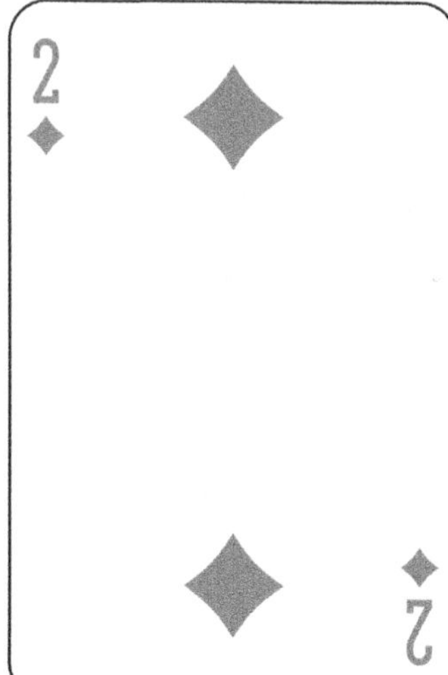

Turn the page when you have memorized the items.

Which Card?

Which one of the following three cards is the missing card in the arrangement below?

Solution on page 151

FIND THE 5 DIFFERENCES

Find the 5 difference between the two pictures.

Solution on page 151

Writing about your life...

What was your favorite job or volunteer experience? Why did you enjoy it? Who did you work with? What tasks did you work on?

ANSWERS

Answers

Page 10: Rhyme Time

Rhymes with "Star"	**Rhymes with "Show"**
are, car, bar, far, jar, par, tar, scar, spar, radar, bazaar, cigar, guitar, jaguar, radar, seminar, registrar, caviar. *Other answers are possible.*	flow, glow, go, grow, dough, crow, stow, throw, tow, toe, snow, row, pro, sew, owe, mow, below, know, throw *Other answers are possible.*

Pages 11-12: Details

1.

2.

Pages 13-14: Particular Pictures

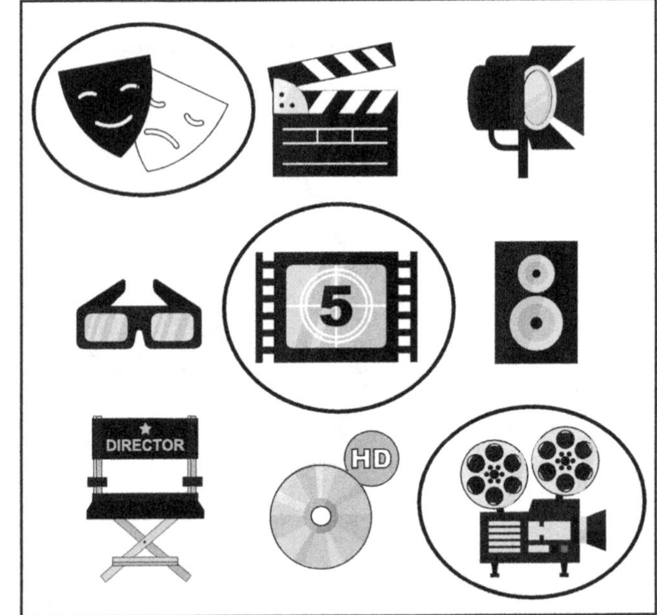

Page 15: Categories

Comedy TV shows

Friends, Three's Company, Bewitched, Family Ties, Frasier, Happy Days....

Many other answers are possible.

Page 15: Categories

Movie Actors
Greta Garbo, Cary Grant, James Stewart, Mae West, Sidney Poitier, Fred Astaire, Tom Cruise, Hugh Jackman, James Dean, Steve Martin, Charlie Chaplin.
Many other answers are possible.

Pages 16-17: Crossword

1 C	O	2 M	M	E	3 R	C	4 I	A	5 L		6 A	R	7 C
O		A			O		N		8 A	N	N		A
9 M	A	R	Y		N		10 G	A	S		11 D	E	N
E		C			12 A	I	R		S		Y		D
D		13 H	14 E	A	L		I		I				Y
Y			A		D		15 D	16 O	E				
			S					R			17 A	18 T	E
19 R	E	N	T		20 G	A	R	A	G	21 E		E	
E					R			N		V		A	
22 B	A	23 L	L		24 O	N		25 G	26 R	E	A	S	E
A		E			O		27 B	E	E			E	
		A			M				A				
28 P	A	R						29 F	L	I	30 G	H	31 T
L		32 N	I	33 G	H	34 T		O			R		H
O				E		A		O			A		E
35 T	H	E	A	T	E	R		36 T	O		37 B	E	N

Page 18: Trivia Matching

1. D. Al Pacino
2. A. Judy Garland
3. G. John Travolta
4. J. Orson Welles
5. H. Gene Kelly
6. B. Humphrey Bogart
7. C. Mark Hamill
8. I. Clark Gable
9. E. James Stewart
10. F. Gregory Peck

Answers

Page 20: Backwards

1. .gnidliub eht tfel sah sivlE
2. .enim sa doog sa si sseug ruoY
3. .ognat ot owt sekat tI
4. .drows eht naht reithgim si nep ehT.

Page 21: Movie Set, Word Search

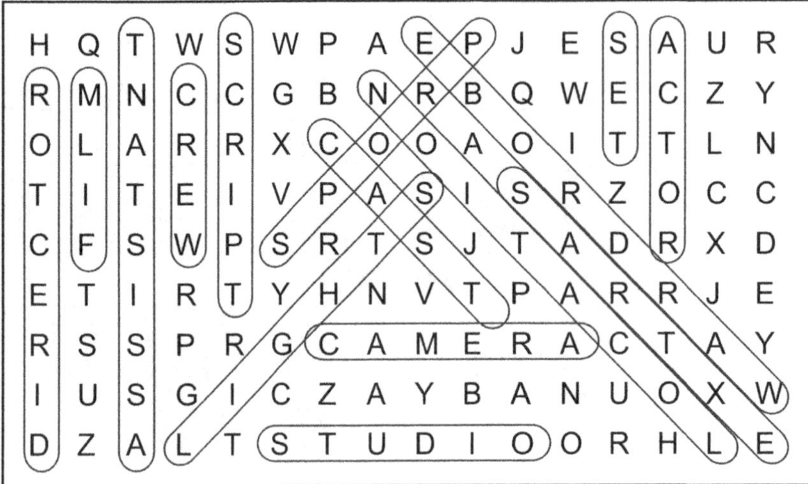

Page 22: Sudoku

8	6	9	7	1	**4**	3	2	**5**
5	7	**3**	2	8	6	4	**1**	9
4	1	2	9	**5**	3	8	7	6
9	**5**	4	6	7	8	**1**	3	2
7	2	6	**3**	4	1	9	5	**8**
1	3	8	5	2	**9**	7	6	4
2	8	5	4	3	7	**6**	9	1
6	**4**	7	1	**9**	2	5	8	**3**
3	9	**1**	**8**	6	5	2	**4**	7

Pages 23-24: Kevin

pizza	fries	**cookies**
popcorn	tape	nachos
juice	**beer**	soda
coffee	wings	gum
taffy	VCR	**DVD**
burgers	**ottoman**	pretzel
chips	glasses	caramel

Pages 23-24: Joy

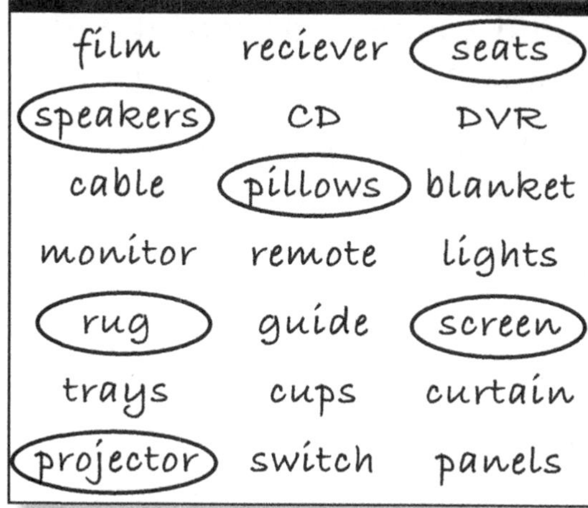

film	reciever	**seats**
speakers	CD	DVR
cable	**pillows**	blanket
monitor	remote	lights
rug	guide	**screen**
trays	cups	curtain
projector	switch	panels

Pages 27-28: Challenge

1. Donkey	5. Cake
2. Apple	6. Bee
3. Car	7. Shovel
4. Ticket	8. House

Page 25: 5 Differences

Page 26: Odd One Out

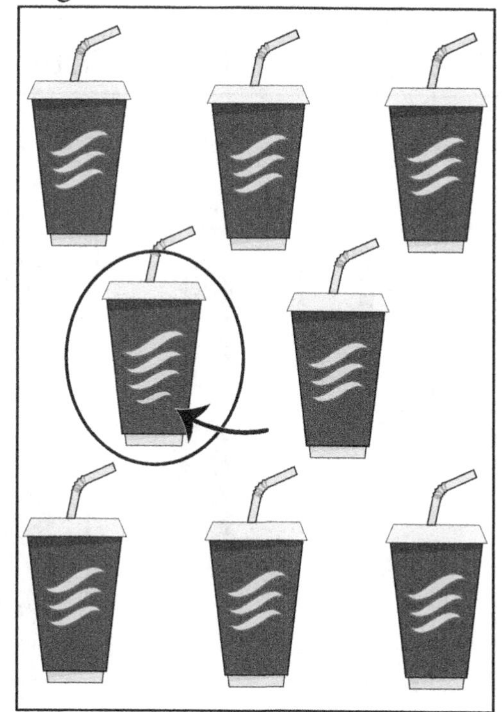

Answers

Page 28: Well Made Words, Letters A, E, V, L, T, G

gavel valet aglet gave vale	veal gale gate late tale	teal vet get leg gal	lag age ale let alt	ate tea at a	*Other words are possible.*

Page 30: Rhyme Time

Rhymes with "Dad"	**Rhymes with "Friend"**
add, bad, chad, clad, fad, plaid, grad, had, lad, mad, pad, rad, sad, scad, tad, dyad, doodad, nomad, ironclad *Other answers are possible.*	bend, blend, end, fend, lend, spend, mend, pretend, trend, send, penned, amend, attend, append, offend, suspend *Other answers are possible.*

Pages 31-32: Particular Pictures

Pages 33-34: Patricia

mittens	scarf	cookies
candle	ring	pen
flowers	watch	sweater
pants	book	hat
candy	sled	skates
doll	puzzle	frame
shoes	ball	tie

Page 36: Sudoku

3	**4**	9	**7**	5	2	1	**6**	8
5	6	8	9	4	**1**	7	2	3
2	7	**1**	6	8	3	**9**	4	5
4	**1**	5	2	**7**	9	8	3	6
8	3	2	**4**	1	6	5	7	**9**
6	9	7	8	3	5	4	**1**	2
9	8	3	1	6	4	2	5	**7**
1	**2**	6	5	**9**	7	3	8	4
7	5	**4**	**3**	2	8	**6**	9	1

Pages 33-34: Scott

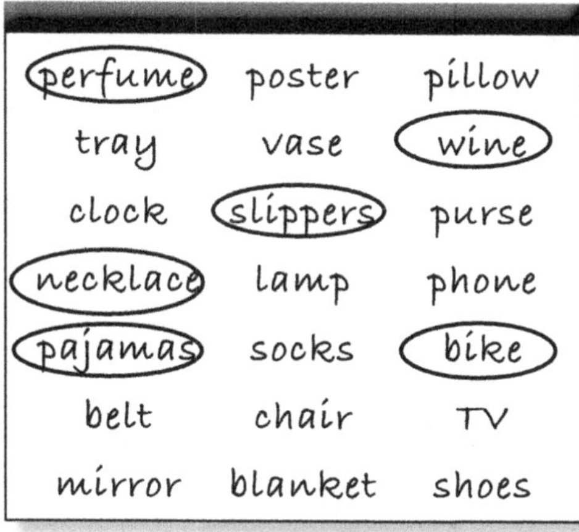

perfume	poster	pillow
tray	vase	wine
clock	slippers	purse
necklace	lamp	phone
pajamas	socks	bike
belt	chair	TV
mirror	blanket	shoes

Page 37: 5 Differences

Page 38: Complete It!

1. need
2. sheep
3. place
4. apple
5. island
6. feather
7. bite
8. heads
9. heart
10. company

Answers

Pages 40-41: Crossword

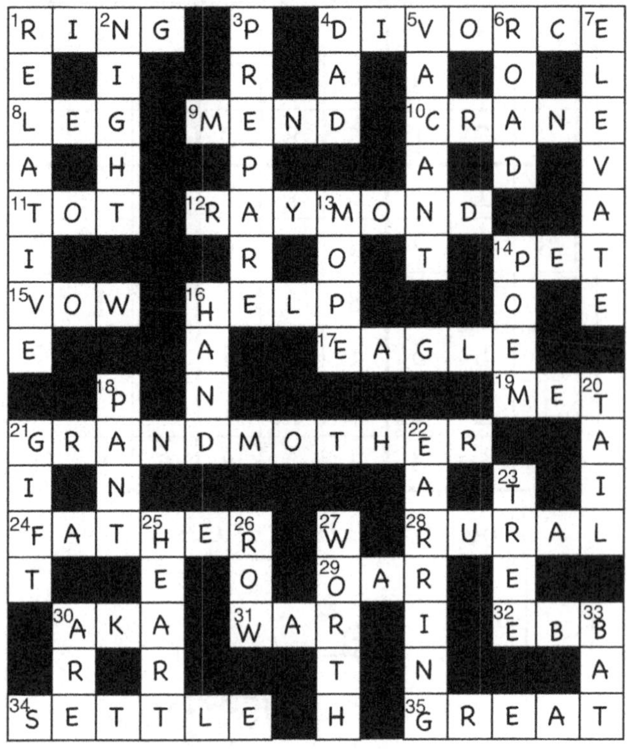

Page 42: Backwards

1. .devlah elbuort a si derahs elbuort A
2. .si traeh eht erehw si emoH
3. .htorb eht liops skooc ynam ooT
4. .esaec reven lliw sredonW

Page 43: Word search

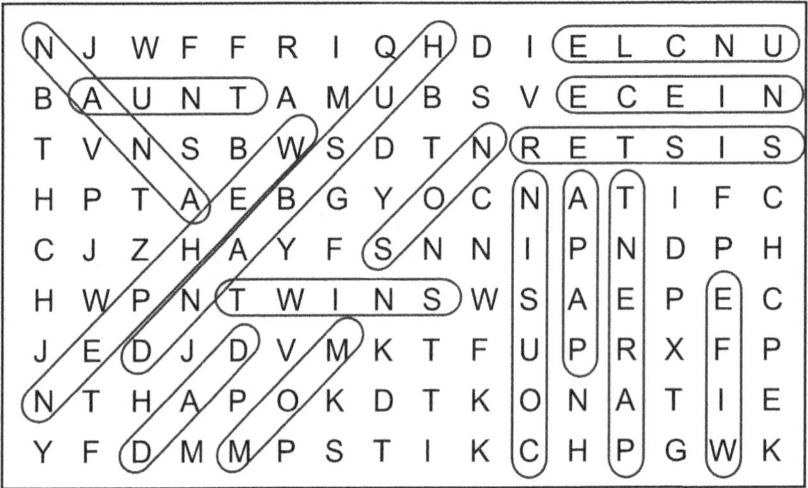

Page 44: Odd One Out

Pages 45-46: Challenge

1. Tooth
2. Ice Cream
3. Cat
4. Road
5. Cup
6. Chair
7. Tree
8. Sweater

Page 46: Well Made Words: Letters M, I, L, B, E, T

limb	belt	bite	elm	let	*Other*
lime	emit	time	met	lit	*words are*
mile	item	blet	bet	tie	*possible.*
bile	mite	tile	bit	be	
melt	mile	lite	lie	it	

Page 48: Rhyme Time

Rhymes with "Soil"	**Rhymes with "Tree"**
boil, coil, spoil, broil, foil, roil, toil, oil, embroil, loyal, royal, turmoil, recoil, disloyal, goyle *Other answers are possible.*	bee, fee, brie, flea, glee, key, knee, plea, sea, see, spree, tea, pee, she, he, we, agree, pea, free, rupee, trustee, TV *Other answers are possible.*

Answers

Pages 49-50: Particular Pictures

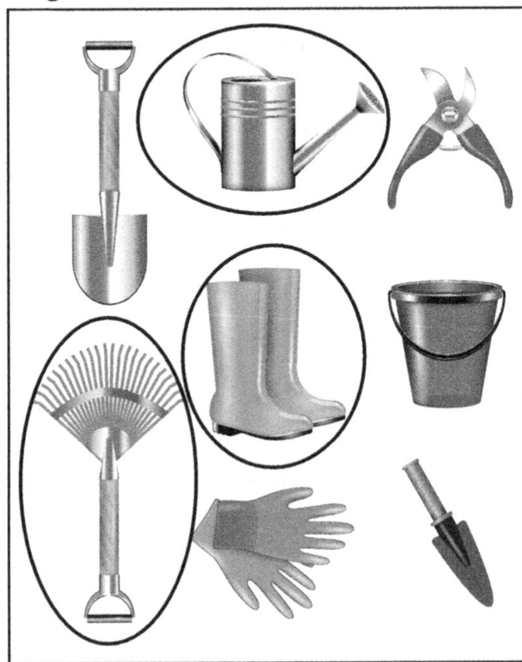

Pages 53-54: Delightful Details

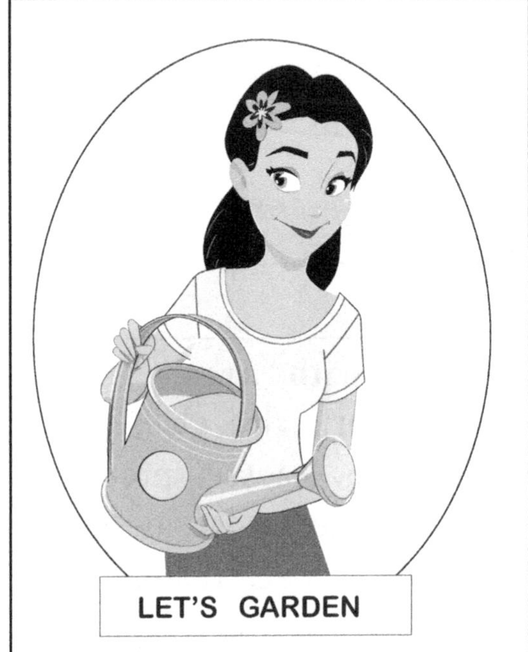

Pages 51-52: Derek

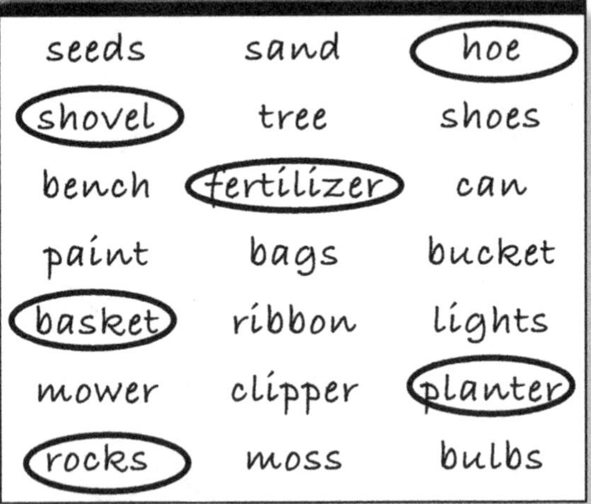

seeds sand hoe
shovel tree shoes
bench fertilizer can
paint bags bucket
basket ribbon lights
mower clipper planter
rocks moss bulbs

Pages 51-52: Susan

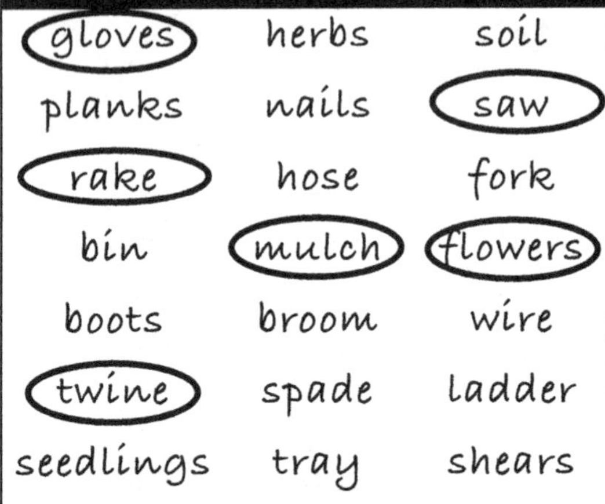

gloves herbs soil
planks nails saw
rake hose fork
bin mulch flowers
boots broom wire
twine spade ladder
seedlings tray shears

Page 55: Cool Categories

Flowers
Daisy, Rose, Poppy, Lily, Foxglove, Pansy, Tulip Orchid, Bluebell, Crocus, Daffodil, Marigold
Many other answers are possible.

Page 55: Cool Categories

Trees

Maple, Juniper, Ash, Aspen, Birch, Elm, Pine, Pear, Apple, Palm, Walnut, Cedar, Spruce, Oak, Poplar, Chestnut, Willow

Many other answers are possible.

Page 56: Sudoku

3	4	9	7	5	**2**	**1**	6	8
5	6	8	9	**4**	1	7	**2**	3
2	**7**	1	6	8	3	9	4	5
4	1	5	**2**	7	9	8	3	6
8	3	**2**	4	1	6	**5**	7	9
6	9	7	8	3	**5**	4	1	**2**
9	**8**	3	1	6	4	2	5	7
1	2	**6**	5	**9**	7	3	**8**	4
7	5	4	**3**	2	8	6	9	**1**

Page 57: Backwards

1. .sesor pu gnimoc si gnihtyrevE
2. .srewolf yaM gnirb srewohs lirpA
3. .wos uoy tahw paer uoY
4. .tiurf sti yb nwonk si eert ehT

Page 59: Landscaping, Word Search

J	D	B	U	S	H	E	S	Y	C	G	S	K	C	E	D
T	L	I	O	S	Z	X	V	T	S	G	I	W	T	E	R
E	T	G	P	A	L	A	I	R	E	T	N	A	L	P	K
T	R	E	L	L	I	S	U	E	T	E	R	C	N	O	C
T	C	W	G	H	Y	N	E	N	S	Y	Y	C	S	B	O
G	W	Y	C	C	H	S	S	A	N	D	Z	S	F	E	I
N	W	N	I	F	E	N	C	E	G	P	A	C	X	Z	T
R	E	J	C	F	D	N	O	P	G	R	Q	N	S	A	A
B	U	F	T	R	E	E	S	Y	G	C	O	G	W	G	P

Answers

Page 60: Odd One Out

Page 62: Letters U, A, D, S, Y, T

dusty	sty	at
study	ads	a
adust	sad	
duty	uta	*Other words are possible.*
days	day	
daut	tad	
stay	tau	
stud	us	
dust	as	
say	ad	
sate	ya	

Pages 61-62: Challenge

1. Violin
2. Bed
3. Window
4. Cookie
5. Bench
6. Rose
7. Book
8. Plate

Page 64: Rhyme Time

Rhymes with "Game"

aim, claim, dame, blame, fame, name, tame, shame, same, acclaim, exclaim, rename, came, plain, frame. *Other answers are possible.*

Rhymes with "Dice"

nice, mice, rice, twice, trice, vice, spice, splice, price, excise, sacrifice, dice, precise, paradise, device, edelweiss. *Other answers are possible.*

Pages 65-66: Particular Pictures

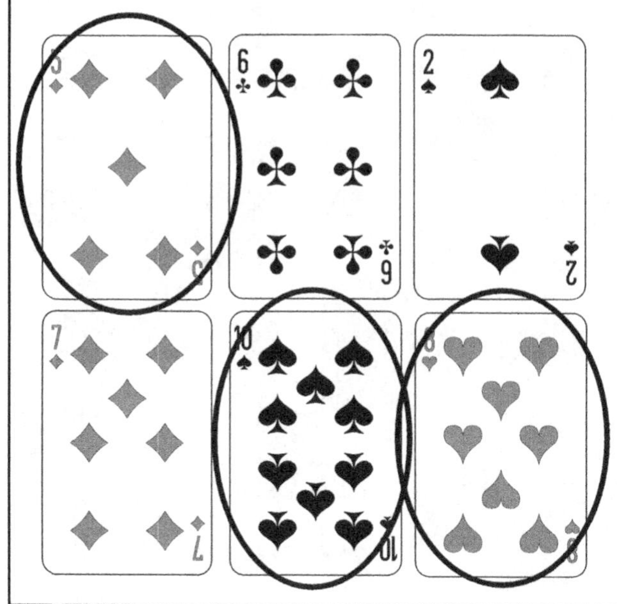

Pages 67-68: Jim

9	81	2	11
7	5	71	9
26	73	64	6
55	1	72	83
76	32	4	42
58	14	6	3

Pages 67-68: Karen

90	2	65	3
68	7	62	5
51	27	47	86
72	54	98	4
24	16	18	93
76	45	4	3

Pages 69-70: Details

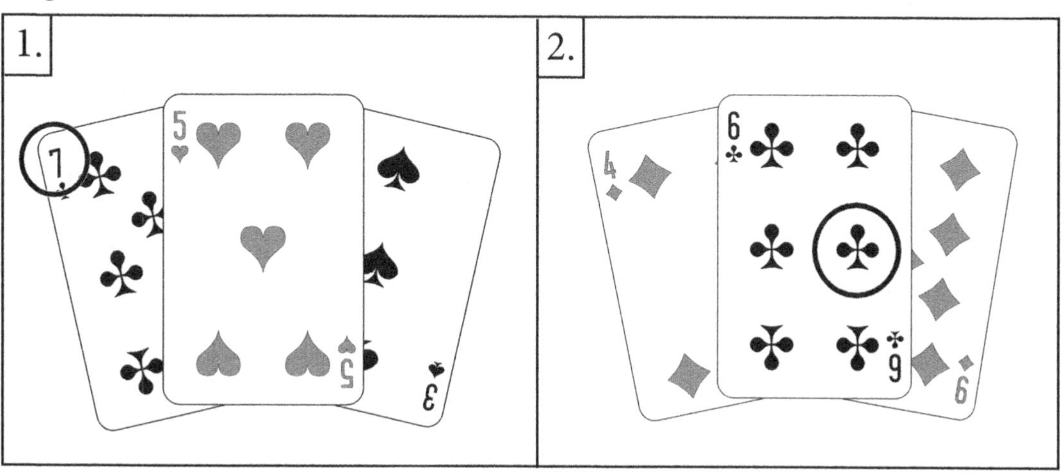

Answers

Page 71: Categories

Card games

Uno, Blackjack, Solitaire Go Fish, Hearts, Rummy, Euchre, Crazy Eights, War, Poker, Old Maid, Cribbage, Canasta, Spades, Bluff, Spoons, Speed. *Many other answers are possible.*

Board Games

Scrabble, Risk, Monopoly, Clue, Battleship, Trivial Pursuit, Operation, Yahtzee, Sorry, Mouse Trap, Cranium, Chutes & Ladders, Life, Trouble, Candy Land. *Many other answers are possible.*

Pages 72-73: Crossword

1 K	I	2 N	G	■	3 P	E	N	■	4 C	A	5 R	D	6 S
I	■	I	■	■	L	■	■	■	O	■	E	■	W
7 T	A	G	■	8 B	A	N	9 A	N	A	■	10 S	E	A
E	■	H	■	■	N	■	N	■	11 T	O	P	■	M
■	■	12 T	13 A	K	E	■	A	■	■	■	E	■	■
14 O	■	■	N	■	15 T	U	G	■	■	■	16 C	A	17 P
18 P	O	T	S	■	■	■	19 R	A	20 P	■	T	■	L
I	■	■	W	■	■	■	A	■	E	■	■	■	A
21 N	A	P	E	■	■	■	M	■	22 P	U	23 P	P	Y
I	■	■	24 R	O	25 P	E	■	■	P	■	E	■	■
26 O	F	F	■	■	R	■	■	■	27 E	A	G	E	28 R
N	■	■	■	■	29 E	N	30 T	E	R	■	■	■	A
■	■	■	31 C	U	P	■	I	■	■	32 S	L	O	B
33 D	E	A	R	■	34 A	E	R	I	A	L	■	■	B
O	■	■	O	■	R	■	E	■	■	O	■	■	I
35 T	R	I	P	■	E	■	D	■	■	36 T	A	R	T

Page 74: Sudoku

2	6	7	**4**	1	5	3	9	8
9	8	1	7	**6**	3	**2**	5	4
5	3	**4**	8	9	**2**	6	1	**7**
1	**5**	3	2	**8**	6	4	7	9
4	9	6	**5**	7	1	8	**3**	2
7	**2**	8	9	3	4	1	**6**	5
3	7	**2**	1	4	9	5	8	**6**
6	4	9	3	**5**	8	7	**2**	1
8	1	5	**6**	2	7	**9**	4	3

Answers

Page 75: Backwards

1. .tsehc ruoy ot esolc sdrac ruoy peeK.
2. .emag nwo rieht ta enoemos taeB
3. .nuf gnivah ruoy nehw seilf emiT
4. .syeknom fo lerrab a naht nuf eroM

Page 77: Fun & Games, Word Search

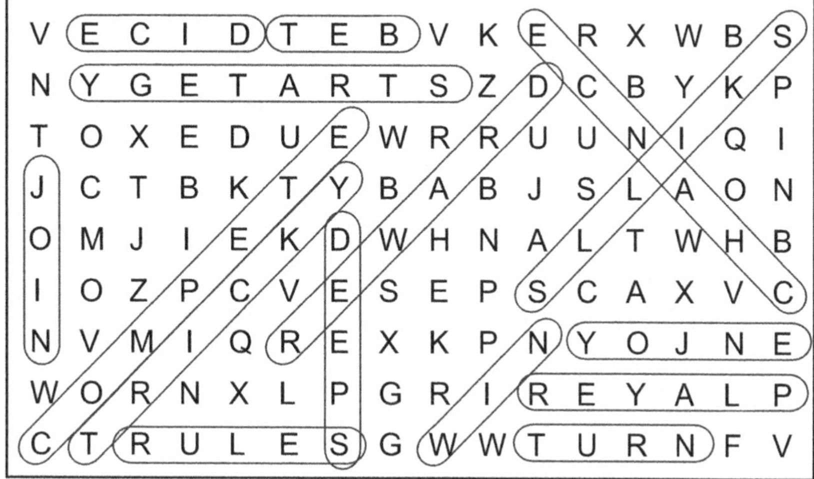

Page 78: Odd One Out

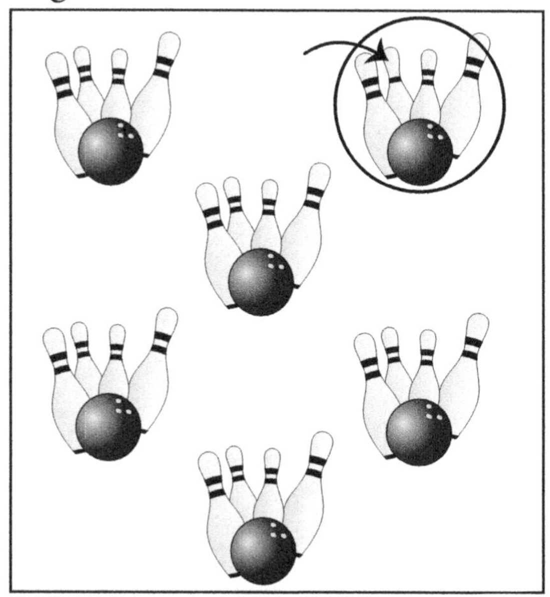

Pages 79-80: Challenge

1. Purse
2. Kangaroo
3. Jam
4. Cup
5. Fence
6. Paper
7. Leaf
8. Stream

Answers

Page 80: Well Made Words, Letters A, C, G, T, R, E

grace	crate	gate	arc	are
cart	acre	tear	cat	tag
cater	race	rate	age	at
react	gear	ace	rag	*Other words*
great	cage	act	get	*are possible.*

Page 82: Rhyme Time

Rhymes with "Trip"	**Rhymes with "Fun"**
clip, nip, rip, lip whip, zip, strip, drip, flip, ship, quip, tip, slip, equip, hip, fingertip, blip, microchip, speakership. *Other answers are possible.*	stun, bun, done, none, won, ton, sun, pun, run, begun, nun, gun, shun, anyone, outrun, undone, spun, one. *Other answers are possible.*

Pages 83-84: Particular Pictures

Pages 85-86: Ray

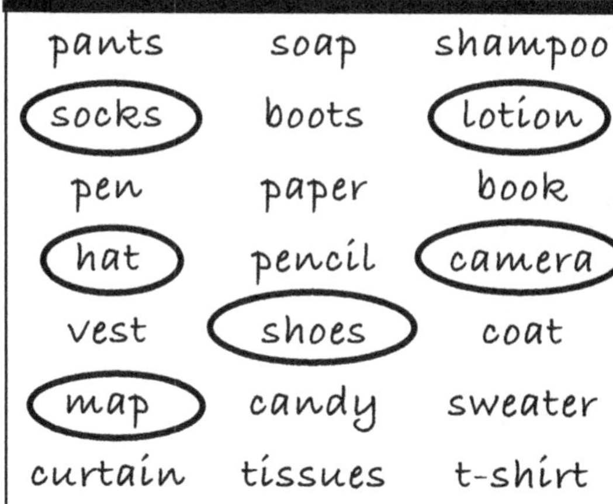

pants soap shampoo
socks boots lotion
pen paper book
hat pencil camera
vest shoes coat
map candy sweater
curtain tissues t-shirt

Pages 85-86: Kim

rope dress journal
shorts skirt sandals
purse watch lamp
matches canoe blanket
bag kayak jacket
net tent mat
pan plate forks

Page 89: Categories

World Cities
London, New York, Toronto, Lisbon, Paris, Berlin, Mexico City, Chicago, Lima, Oslo, Rome, Athens. *Many other answers are possible.*

Pages 87-88: Delightful Details

Page 89: Categories

Landmarks
Big Ben, Sydney Opera House, Stonehenge, Great Wall of China, Taj Mahal, The Great Sphinx, Colosseum, Statue of Liberty, CN Tower, Acropolis of Athens, Eiffel Tower, Leaning Tower of Pisa, Golden Gate Bridge, London Eye. *Many other answers are possible.*

Answers

Page 90: Sudoku

8	7	9	4	1	**2**	3	**5**	6
6	1	4	**5**	3	8	7	9	2
5	**2**	3	6	9	7	**4**	8	1
9	4	1	8	**6**	3	2	**7**	5
3	5	**7**	9	2	4	6	1	**8**
2	8	6	**1**	7	5	9	4	3
1	**3**	2	7	8	**9**	5	6	**4**
4	9	8	**3**	5	6	1	**2**	7
7	6	5	2	**4**	1	**8**	3	9

Page 91: Backwards

1. .dnim eht snedaorb levarT.
2. .kcart netaeb eht ffO
3. .aes gninihs ot aes morF
4. .esactius a fo tuo eviL

Page 92: Ski Trip, Word Search

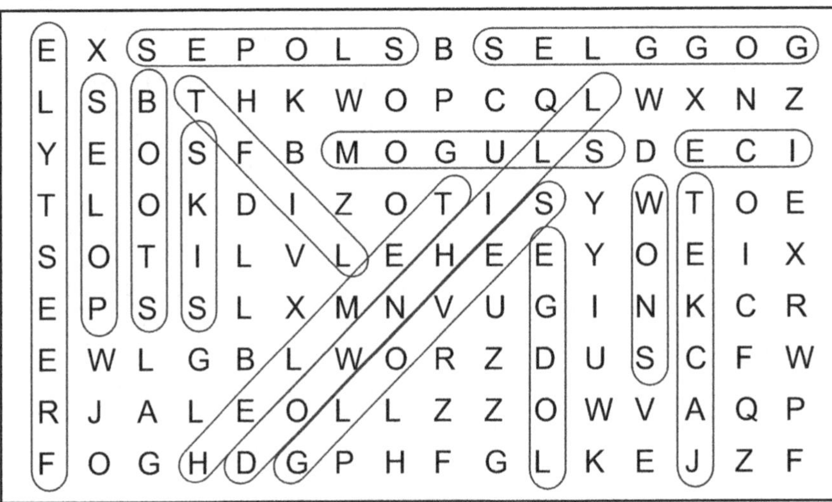

Page 94: Odd One Out

Pages 95-96 Challenge

1. Racket
2. Grass
3. Dress
4. Car
5. Scarf
6. Banana
7. Bowl
8. Bear

Page 96: Letters F, R, B, A, I, Y

fairy	rib	if
fray	ria	ab
fair	far	a
barf	air	*Other*
airy	bay	*words are*
bray	far	*possible.*
fry	rif	
bar	bra	
fib	fir	
fab	yar	
ray	by	

Page 98: Rhyme Time

Rhymes with "Brush"

crush, hush, blush, flush, lush, rush, shush, mush, thrush, slush, sagebrush, plush, gush, aflush. *Other answers are possible.*

Rhymes with "Draw"

awe, blah, craw, flaw, jaw, thaw, slaw, spa, paw, law, thaw, ma, pa, hoopla, jigsaw, maw, seesaw, Utah, gnaw.

Other answers are possible.

Answers

Page s99-100 Particular Pictures

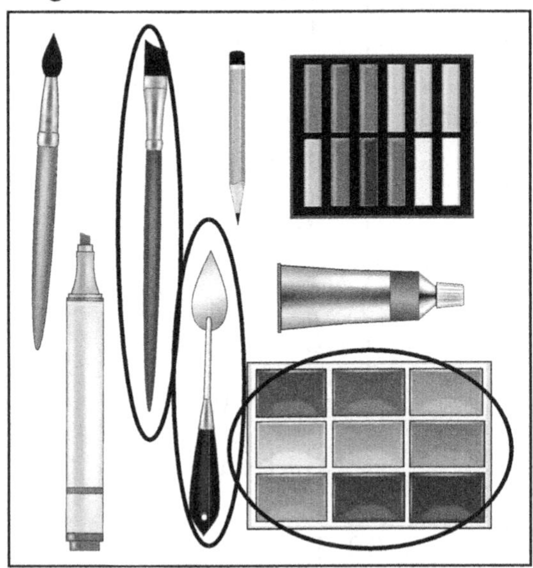

Pages 103-4: Particular Pictures

Pages 101-102: Cory

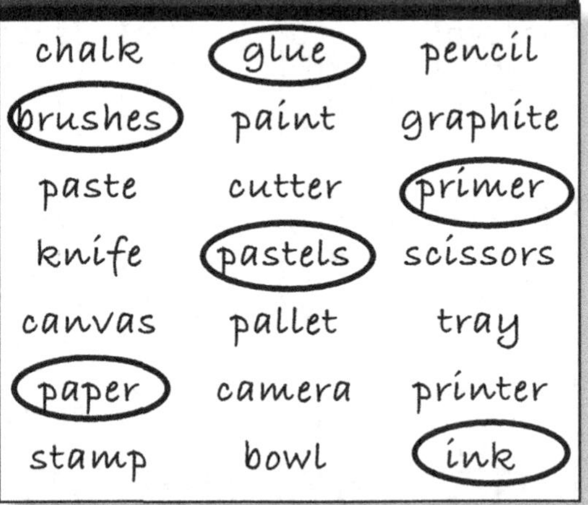

Pages101-102: Trudie

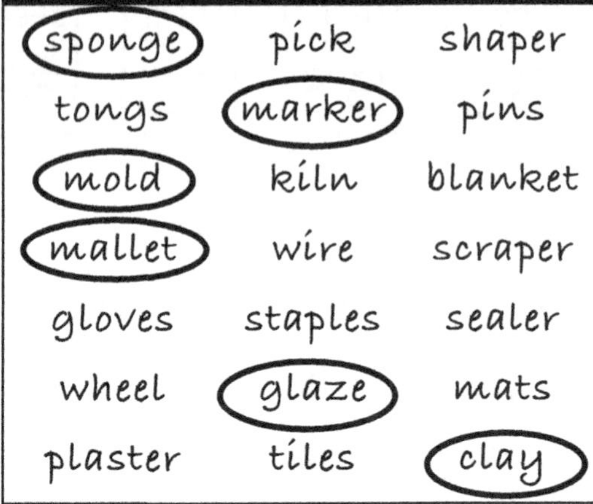

Page 105: Categories

Artists
Donatello, Pablo Picasso, Edgar Degas, Paul Cézanne, Henri Matisse, Paul Klee, Diego Rivera, Norman Rockwell. *Many other answers are possible.*

Page 105: Categories

Art Galleries

The Smithsonian, MoMA, Le Louvre, Metropolitan Museum of Art, The British Museum, The Prado, , The Uffizi Gallery, Tate Modern. *Many other answers are possible.*

Page 106: Sudoku

1	**9**	3	4	**7**	2	5	6	8
2	7	8	5	6	**1**	4	9	**3**
4	6	5	**8**	9	3	**2**	1	7
7	2	6	1	5	**9**	3	8	4
8	**4**	9	**2**	3	6	1	**7**	5
3	5	**1**	7	**4**	8	9	2	**6**
5	3	2	6	1	**7**	8	4	9
6	8	**4**	9	**2**	5	**7**	3	1
9	**1**	7	3	8	4	6	**5**	2

Page 107: Backwards

1. .sdrow dnasuoth a throw si erutcip A
2. .renroc a otni flesruoy tniaP
3. .senil eht edistuo roloC
4. .krow thgil ekam sdnah ynaM

Page 109: Sculpture, Word Search

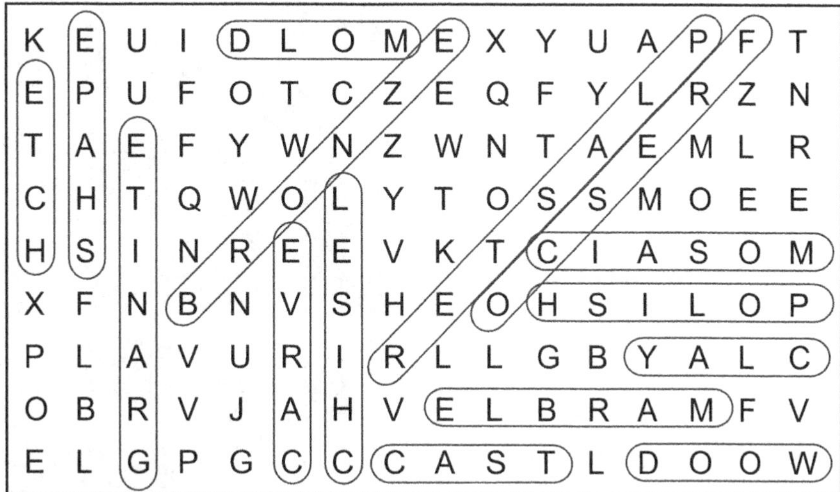

Answers

Page 110: Odd One Out

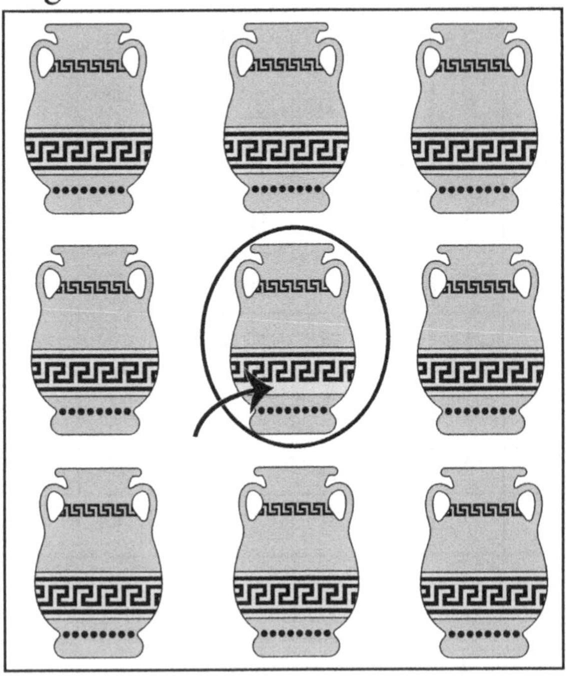

Pages 111-112: Challenges

1. Phone
2. Mouse
3. Basket
4. Candy
5. Sock
6. Stick
7. Rope
8. Bicycle

Page 112: P, R, T, I, B, E

tribe	rib
tripe	pie
biter	bit
bear	pit
bite	tip
bit	rip
pier	tie
ripe	be
trip	pi
tire	it
pert	I
tier	*Other words*
bet	*are possible.*

Pages 114-115: Crossword

1 C	A	2 M	E	R	3 A		4 G	I	5 R	A	F	6 F	7 E
A		A			U		O		E			8 O	N
9 M	O	R	E		G		10 L	O	S	E		11 A	T
E		R			U		D		T		12 A	L	E
13 L	A	Y			S						P		R
			14 A	N	T		15 S	U	N		R		
16 F	O	U	R				L			17 B	I	L	18 L
L			19 T	20 R	I	P	O	D			L		O
21 O	U	22 R		O			W						U
U		E		S				23 M	24 A	I	25 L	E	D
R		L		26 E	A	R	27 N		N		O		E
		I					E		28 N	29 O	W		R
30 B	L	A	N	31 D			V			T			
E		B		U			E		32 S	T	A	N	33 D
S		L		34 S	O	U	R			E			A
35 T	R	E	A	T					36 B	R	A	I	N

Page 116: Dancing, Word Search

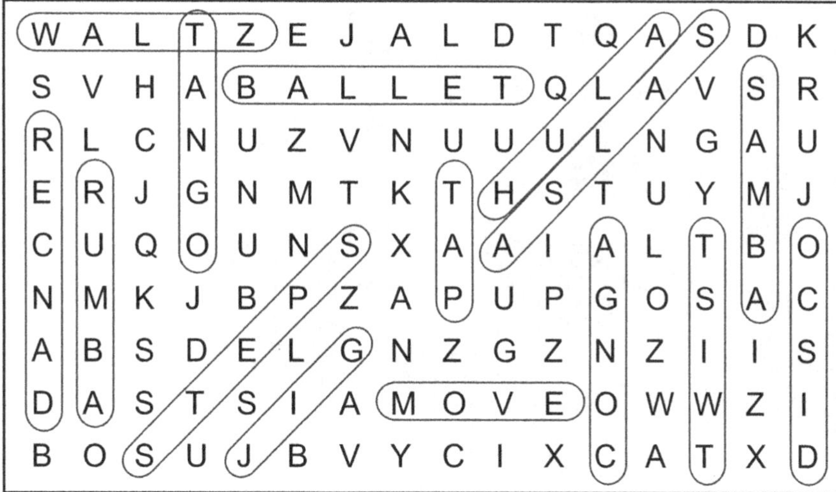

Pages 117-118: Which Card?

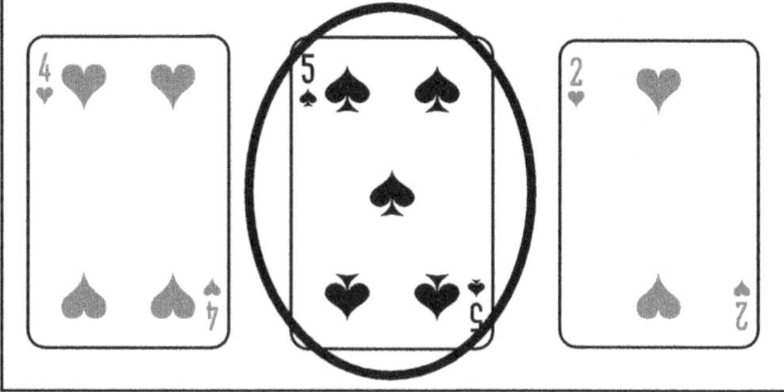

Page 119: 5 Differences

Answers

Pages 120-121: Crossword

1 O	N	2 I	O	N		3 H	I	D	4 E		5 B	A	6 T
C		N				E			7 A	I	R		H
8 T	O	N	G	S		9 L	I	10 A	R		A		I
O		O				P		11 I	N		12 I	N	N
P		13 C	O	O	K	S		S			N		K
14 U	S	E						L					
S		N		15 S				16 E	A	17 R			18 G
		19 T	20 A	I	L	O	21 R			U			A
			L				U			22 N	23 E	A	R
24 R	E	N	T		25 A		I				A		B
A			26 E	R	R	A	N	27 D			G		A
28 I	T		R		E			A			29 E	G	G
S				30 I				31 Y	E	32 A	R		E
33 I	N	34 S	I	D	E			S		N			
N		A		O						N			35 I
36 S	A	D	D	L	E			37 S	H	A	R	E	D

Page 122: Countries, Word Search

H	P	O	R	T	U	G	A	L	Y	N	A	M	R	E	G
V	Z	C	I	G	R	E	E	C	E	U	W	L	T	F	I
R	N	P	A	C	A	I	D	N	I	D	Y	Q	K	R	T
Y	N	W	A	N	B	X	M	A	N	L	L	A	E	A	E
A	I	W	P	Z	A	B	X	A	Y	M	I	L	J	N	K
W	A	Z	E	J	X	D	L	L	Q	V	A	Z	A	C	A
R	P	S	R	L	A	G	A	M	V	N	G	P	A	E	T
O	S	S	U	X	N	T	C	E	D	N	A	P	Q	R	B
N	Z	M	B	E	I	A	S	U	L	J	D	C	I	M	B

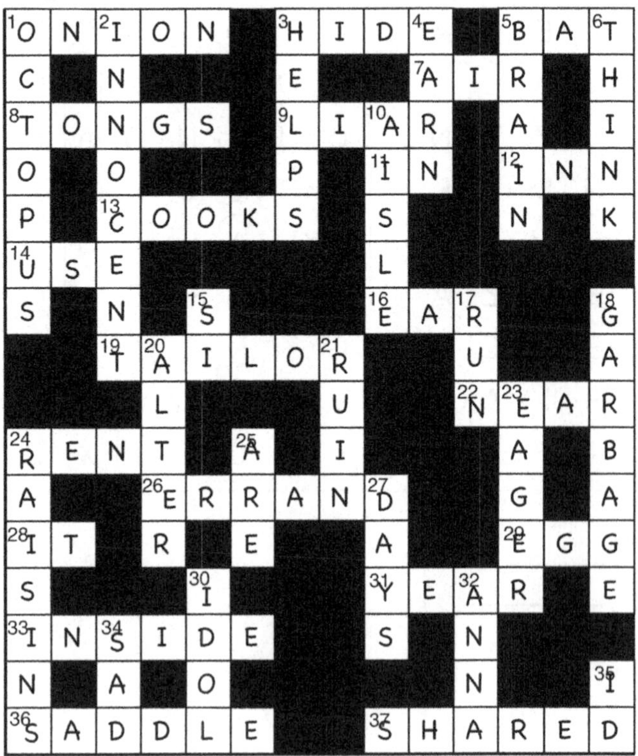

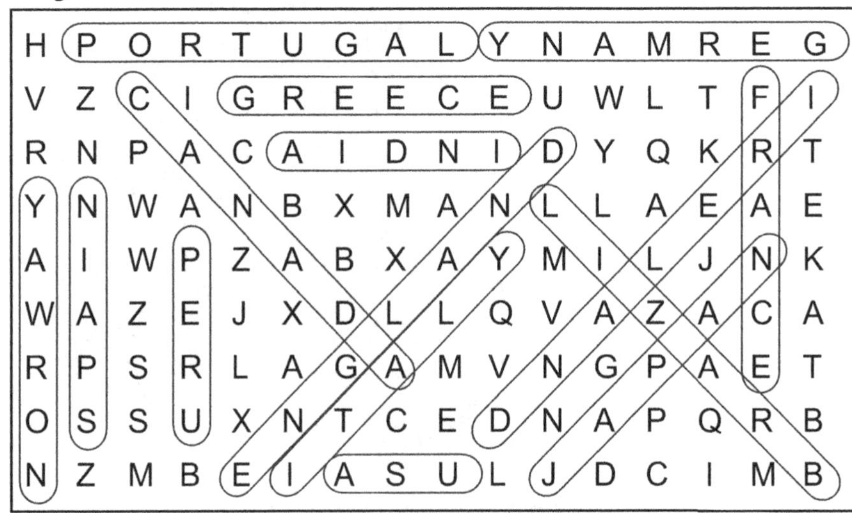

Answers

Pages 123-124 Which Card?

Page 125: 5 Differences

For more puzzle books please check out:

www.LomicBooks.com

Thank you!